# ACTING WALES
## STARS of STAGE and SCREEN

# ACTING WALES
## STARS of STAGE and SCREEN

Peter Stead

University of Wales Press
Cardiff 2002

**British Library Cataloguing-in-Publication Data**
A catalogue record for this book is available from the British Library.

ISBN 0–7083–1623–9

Designed by Neil James Angove
Typeset at University of Wales Press
Printed in Great Britain by The Bath Press

# Contents

# Preface

This volume of distinctly subjective essays has grown out of decades of theatre and cinema attendance but also, as will be evident, out of a lifelong love of good reviewing. I love the debate on acting and I thank all those many critics whose words I have used and acknowledged. Over the years I have often discussed the stars of stage and screen with Norman Stead, Dai Smith and Berwyn Rowlands and I thank them for their particular enthusiasms. I owe an enormous debt of gratitude to Geraint Stanley Jones, my chair at Sgrîn, who encouraged me throughout and then provided a splendid final critique that rectified significant omissions. Chris Mason provided timely practical assistance whilst at the Press Susan Jenkins and her colleagues were remarkably patient and always encouraging. Above all else I must thank my wife Elizabeth for her energy, common sense, technical skills, literary know-how and love without all of which this book would not have been started, let alone finished.

Peter Stead
Swansea, Summer 2002

# Acknowledgements

The photographs in this book have been reproduced by kind permission of the following:

BBC: Windsor Davies, p.147 (*It Ain't Half Hot Mum*).
Buena Vista International: Matthew Rhys, p.159 (*Titus*).
Canal+ Image UK Ltd.: Hugh Griffith, p.83 (*Lucky Jim*), Kenneth Griffith, p.93 (*Only Two Can Play*), Stanley Baker, p.59 (*The Cruel Sea*).
Carlton International Media Ltd./LFI: Ivor Novello, p.17 (*The Lodger*), Rachel Roberts, p.71 (*This Sporting Life*).
Columbia: 'On Acting', p.1 (*The Guns of Navarone*), Catherine Zeta Jones, p.175 (*The Mask of Zorro*), Anthony Hopkins, pp. i, iii and jacket (*The Remains of the Day*).
Granada: Ioan Gruffudd, pp. i, iii and jacket (*Hornblower*).
The Harvard Theatre Collection: Emlyn Williams, p.31 (as Charles Dickens).
Laurence Burns/ArenaPAL: Jonathan Pryce, p.131 (*Hamlet*).
London Films Production: Siân Phillips, pp. i, iii and jacket (*I, Claudius*).
Richard Attenborough Productions: Anthony Hopkins, p.105 (*Shadowlands*).
S4C: Ioan Gruffudd, p.185 (*Solomon a Gaenor*), Philip Madoc and Hywel Bennett, p.147 (*A Mind to Kill*)
Twentieth Century Fox: Richard Burton, p.45 (*Cleopatra*).
Universal Studios: Rhys Ifans, p.159 (*Twin Town*).
Western Mail & Echo Ltd.: Siân Phillips, p.121 (as Marlene Dietrich), Glyn Houston, p.147 (photographer Mike Alsford).

Every effort has been made to secure the permission of copyright holders to reproduce images.

# $O$n Acting

I recall vividly the moment I first consciously thought about actors. The school had taken us to a local cinema to see Laurence Olivier's film *Richard III*. Olivier himself, of course, was memorable and his grotesque, leering depiction of the king was a few years later to inspire my only nightmare: I was to awake shouting 'It's the Devil, it's the Devil', as Olivier's Richard beat at the bedroom window. During the first viewing of the film, however, it was the actor playing Richmond who prompted thoughts on the nature of the profession. The part was played with a deliberate dark intensity and an irresistible energy; none of us was surprised that this character ended up killing Richard and becoming king himself as Henry VII. What had amazed us, though, was that this Earl of Richmond had a Welsh accent – not a posh, Sunday afternoon BBC Welsh accent but a Valleys' accent. We snooty grammar school boys actually roared with laughter when Richmond spoke the line 'Conduct him to his regiment.' He sounded like a Rhondda police sergeant and we had never realized that kind of thing was allowed in serious films. Who was this Stanley Baker?

Almost exclusively the actors in our lives were American, and they were as familiar to us as our next-door neighbours. For the most part these people belonged in their films; we were not particularly interested in them in any other context and we certainly never thought of them as having been paid to do a job. Magazines and Christmas film annuals tried to interest us in how they were discovered working in drugstores or showed them in swimwear by their pools or barbecues, but we were never convinced by those 'snaps', not least because the rich colours seemed artificial and the tanned faces quite unnatural. We were happier with the huge black and white images on screen. We knew all their names and we had our favourites. From the outset my idol was Gregory Peck, largely because he had starred in the movie *Captain Hornblower*, a story I knew thanks to a radio serial. I loved his voice and his slow, measured, thoughtful manner. I would have been happy if this man had been my father or my minister or my political leader, and happier still if I could have been him. Aged about nine I gave a female cousin my portrait and signed it 'Gregery Peck'.

Not that there was any danger of my becoming an actor myself. I was immensely envious when about a quarter of my junior school class frequently paraded out to rehearse their parts as fairies in a local production of *A Midsummer Night's Dream*, but sought consolation in my right-back position in the football team. It was in grammar school that I first became aware of how much acting talent there was around me and of how much work and practice was needed to refine it. At the annual eisteddfod we sat transfixed as senior boys went flat out to win the peroration prize.

We watched and listened so intently that we soon had 'the Quality of Mercy' and 'All the World's a Stage' speeches off pat ourselves. To this day I can see that fair-haired prefect giving every emphasis to 'Sans teeth, sans eyes, sans taste, sans everything'. Incredibly, the school hall was silenced. Even more impressive was the way in which those same reciters brought school plays alive. On these occasions we entered the school hall a little reluctantly, half hoping that things would go wrong and fully hoping that any girls borrowed from the girls' school would be worth the entrance money. The *Tartuffe* I saw at Barry and the *Twelfth Night* at Gowerton were by a long distance the best productions of those plays I have ever seen, fresher and more inventive than subsequent professional efforts. A thoughtful *Murder in the Cathedral* at Swansea's Bishop Gore School had been thrillingly acted, whilst the Helen in Llanelli Grammar School's *Doctor Faustus* not only sank a thousand ships but broke two hundred hearts, inflicting particular pain on those of us who, on the bus back to Gowerton, were told that she was a master's wife.

It was clear at an early stage that I was destined for a passive role as far as school drama was concerned, but I did at least submit to the peroration coaching. I was to recite the first chapter of John's gospel in an important service at my Baptist chapel. Thus it happened that in the front room of a Barry council house an elderly spinster put me through the most brutal moments of my educational career. Within two minutes I was told that I spoke ten times too quickly, that I swallowed consonants and did not finish sentences. We took two hours over the first verse: the 'Word' was indeed God. The whole of a subsequent session was devoted to 'the darkness comprehendeth it not', a phrase I still take care to avoid. In essence I had been deconstructed during those invaluable sessions. The experience put me off acting for life but without Miss Adams I would have done no public speaking at all. A few years later I was asked to play one of the leads in the school play and remembering my trouble with 'comprehendeth it not' I declined. My acting days were over before they had begun, but I was never to lose my interest in those brave souls who were not afraid to be put through the mill of training as they made acting their lives.

It was at Stratford that I was to encounter the full magic of theatre. In 1958 the school took us to see *Hamlet* and *Much Ado About Nothing*, a perfect combination of tragedy and wit that might tempt any adolescent into an interest in professional productions of Shakespeare. The plays were excellent, but there was something else that I recall from that first visit. In a bookshop window I saw a history of Shakespearean acting that was subtitled 'From Burbage to Burton'. It was a moment in which many things fell into place and new arenas of thought opened up. Richard Burbage, I knew, had acted with and for Shakespeare and had been the great hero of the Elizabethan theatre. Richard Burton was from Port Talbot and I had already heard of the impact he had made at Stratford and, more particularly, at the Old Vic earlier in the decade. For me, however, he was essentially a film star whom I had seen first in *The Robe* and then in *Alexander the Great*. Clearly he was Welsh, although a good deal posher than Stanley Baker, but even more he was an exotic, a man in a tunic with curly hair and an undeniably Mediterranean skin texture. Not until that moment at the bookshop had I realized that there was an identifiable tradition of great English acting and that Burton was legitimately seen as the latest star to take his place in a line-up of great names. I had not understood how good he had been and how, just a few years earlier, destiny, or at least a knighthood, had beckoned.

Knighthoods, of course, were the most obvious public expression of how the nation valued great acting. From the outset I associated the honour with what went on at Stratford. *Hamlet* was my first serious play and in the title role was Michael Redgrave. What I observed was a tall, shy man speaking the lines beautifully. Only in later years did I read the comments of those critics who pointed out that there would not be many more fifty-year-old actors taking on the part of the student prince. His presence on the stage had not surprised me: he was a well-known star whom I had seen inventing bouncing bombs in the role of Barnes Wallis in the film *The Dam Busters*. When Redgrave was knighted just a few months after we had seen his Hamlet (and incidentally his Benedick) my school felt that it had played a part in the process. But my interest in the status of great actors was to be sustained in the year of that Redgrave knighthood by another Stratford visit. This time I saw the devil himself: Olivier was there playing Coriolanus, diving to his death and being caught by the heels. Here indeed was the nation's greatest and most charismatic actor, thrilling us with his acrobatics after revealing all his skills in telling his mother to chide him no more for 'I am going to the market place'. It was no surprise to learn that Olivier had been a knight since 1947 and that he personally had never doubted that he was the latest champion to hold the mantle and title of the greatest English actor in direct line of descent from Burbage, Garrick and Kean. Much later I was greatly amused by the information that Olivier had never understood why Ralph Richardson had beaten him to the 'K'. On that visit I was somewhat saddened to learn that Edith Evans, who played Volumnia, mother to Coriolanus, a Dame of the British Empire since 1946, was not directly Welsh. There was to be consolation later when I saw on the London stage Dame Gwen Ffrangcon-Davies, who had decades earlier worked with Shaw and who represented a long chapter of theatre history. She, of course, was the daughter of a famous Welsh father, the singer David Ffrangcon-Davies.

Returning to Wales from that second visit to Stratford I now little doubted that 'the play's the thing'. Together, Olivier as Coriolanus and the American Sam Wanamaker, who had been Iago to Paul Robeson's Othello, had eclipsed Hollywood and, in particular, the Wild West in my imagination. Shakespeare in performance was compelling and addictive. Stratford itself was steeped in history and I very much wanted to read about great performances in earlier decades; I greatly regretted having missed them all. Meanwhile, as an A-level student of English in the process of learning vast chunks of *Macbeth* and *Twelfth Night*, I readily assumed that I was becoming caught up in the mainstream of national culture. The cinema belonged to a street culture that I was leaving behind: I was now becoming a scholar with an interest in theatre, the art form that sustained the national heritage and somehow seemed to establish the country's cultural status. It was all very respectable and those knighthoods and DBEs seemed to confirm that.

Only with further reading did I realize that originally the award of public honours to actors had been a deliberate attempt to offset prejudices against theatre. Theatre, it seemed, was a truly ancient art form and one which had always been regarded with a certain ambivalence. 'All theatre', suggests Robin May, 'springs from the same ultimate and universal source, the religious dances of primitive peoples.' That religious element seemed most evident to me in the way that the English seemed to treat theatres like churches; we entered with awe and never ceased to be reverent. No wonder that leading directors were tempted to deepen the implications. Tyrone Guthrie argues that 'the theatre makes its effect by ritual' and that in all drama 'there is some attempt, rarely conscious, to relate the participants to God', whilst Peter Brook seemed concerned to use his productions to chart the ancient philosophical essentials of space and movement. Why was it then that throughout the centuries so many religious and political leaders had feared theatre and sought to suppress or control it? Clearly, as places of entertainment, theatres had been associated not only with loose living and over-indulgence but also with radical or alternative ideas. This dual perspective on theatre generally was even more pronounced when it came to the position of actors themselves. Roland Barthes was one of a number of writers who had pointed to the priestly origins of acting but, if those first actors had essentially been communicating with the spirit world and therefore transcending their own identities, were they not, as Brian Bates was to argue, essentially operating as shamans? Extending the point, the writer Roger Lewis has suggested that by snatching the identity of others those early actors, hidden behind their masks and make-up, were meddling with dangerous forces. 'Acting', says Lewis, 'is diabolism', and indeed there were occasions in the history of British theatre when the performances of Edmund Kean, Henry Irving and, as I could testify, Laurence Olivier were to bear that out. No wonder that the cautious and conservative were afraid of actors and tried to marginalize them in the culture. There were to be many denunciations and Ian McIntyre has highlighted one of the most comprehensive. In 1757 an anonymous author maintained that 'play-actors are the most profligate wretches and the vilest vermine that hell ever vomited out'. What is more, this critic continued, 'they are the filth and garbage of the earth, the scum and stain of human nature, the excrements and refuse of all mankind, the pests and plagues of human society, the debauchees of men's minds and morals'.

In England, theatre had struggled hard to come in from the fringe. Very largely this process whereby outsiders became insiders was one that acknowledged that the nation's literary heritage in the form of classic drama could not be left entirely in the hands of showmen and mere entertainers. Theatre people had to be recognized as bastions of the national heritage. But there was more to it than that, for the sheer power and romance of the great actors created their own remorseless pressure for wider recognition and acclaim. When the poet Samuel Coleridge wrote possibly the most famous sentence in the history of English theatre criticism he was establishing a hallmark for English acting and creating an expectation that was to excite successive generations of theatre-goers. For Coleridge, to see Edmund Kean act was 'like reading Shakespeare by flashes of lightning'. That sensation was what subsequent Victorian audiences wanted to experience when they went to see Macready and Irving (who became the first theatre knight in 1895). By the end of the century and the beginning of the next the great actor-managers like Sir Johnston Forbes-Robertson, Sir Herbert Tree, Sir Frank Benson and Sir John Martin-Harvey were fulfilling similar expectations. This was the tradition that was given a new lease of life by Richardson, Olivier and Gielgud in the 1940s and it was to prompt the 1950s critic Kenneth Tynan into a fascination with the romantic dimensions of the nation's acting. He encouraged his readers to appreciate the sheer physicality of the panther-like Olivier, and it was he more than anyone who considered similar physical dimensions in the acting of Paul Scofield and Richard Burton, the next obvious theatrical knights, as it seemed then. Throughout the many eras of this acting tradition it became clear that the appeal of leading players was to a far wider public than ever saw them in the flesh. Society generally picked up on the reaction of critics and took a great interest and pleasure in the existence of these personalities. There seemed to be a need for them.

Yet in the 1950s it was apparent that this tradition of great actors was not enough, for classic theatre was but one strand in the national culture. Theatre generally was overwhelmingly dominated by the middle classes and by their middlebrow tastes. The West End and the many provincial repertory theatres had settled down to a well-established diet of romantic comedies, country-house dramas and farce that seemed far removed from reality as perceived by most people. The great challenge facing the theatre was whether it could tackle contemporary issues and in so doing attract new audiences. Meanwhile, in the post-war years cinema had its great moment of glory and had captured a huge audience. Most of the time the people who went to the cinema watched American films and they were very happy with that fact. If asked to name their favourite actors most would immediately come up with American names. There was an honourable place for British films and there was an affection for some British stars but few cinema-goers doubted that as far as film was concerned the home-grown product was but a supporting feature. Hollywood all too clearly spent more money on its product, told good stories, effortlessly bypassed the issues of class and ideology and peopled its films with an endless supply of attractive, charming, witty and utterly natural actors. The challenge for British cinema was whether it could develop a new breed of actors prepared to accept cinematic rather than West End conventions and capable of relating to the new youth phenomenon already being manifested in music.

It was in every respect a crucial era for the performing arts in Britain and, if there was never to be a total outright victory for domestic theatre and cinema, there were at least many honourable achievements. In the theatre there was to be new writing, exciting new companies and a new generation of actors, many from unconventional backgrounds, although, with the closure of many provincial theatres, live drama remained a minority interest and London became even more dominant. There was a new cinema, too, and at long last some critics were able to greet the dawn of British realism, but audiences did not seem impressed with northern settings and dialect and the films still showed their literary origins and the actors their theatrical training. Albert Finney, with possibly more than one eye on Marlon Brando, was consciously attempting to launch a new era in the annals of British film acting, but in this respect the Celts Richard Harris, Stanley Baker and Rachel Roberts were making more telling contributions. In this transitional era London-based film directors travelled north with their actors for location shooting in Halifax, whilst stage plays were televised live in stiflingly hot studios with actors sweating out their anger. It was nevertheless television which was ultimately to scoop the prize as it moved into a dominant position in British culture: in effect it became the equivalent of what the movies had been in America. All the while it fed off symbiotic relationships with the other performing arts. Theatre retained its prestige especially in the form of the two great subsidized companies, and film, surviving crisis after crisis, nevertheless came up with an occasional box-office success or art-house masterpiece. But in every respect television was king. One huge source of regret was that the early tradition of television drama did not survive; the networks were not interested in single dramas chiefly because they had decided that audiences reacted only to series. The hallmark of British television became soaps, sitcoms, costume drama and police series, all of which made it apparent that the culture had caught up with what the Americans had accomplished in their movies a generation earlier. It was now possible for British actors to convey every social nuance in an utterly natural way. Television barmaids were as real as those in one's local and television cops were frighteningly authentic. The charm of this new generation of actors not only allowed them to become national personalities but also created a sense that they were actually playing a part in the real lives of many individuals and families who had become hooked on televised fictions. Television acting had become one of the triumphs of the culture and was characterized by a style, energy, confidence and professionalism that seemed elusive in other walks of British life. In London's West End the knighthoods were still on offer and there were regularly electrifying performances at the pinnacle of live drama, but before the show and during the intervals members of the audience consulted their programmes and joyfully reported that sundry supporting players had appeared in episodes of *Morse*, *The Bill* and *Casualty*.

The British now live in a space heavily peopled with actors, perhaps more than Americans do. The two countries illustrate the manner in which dramatic art and performance occupy different positions and roles in different cultures. These differences are very real, even allowing for the remarkable cross-fertilization. Certain kinds of Englishness are either damned or lauded in the States whilst in the UK the faintest trickle of anti-American criticism is usually drowned by a continuing fascination with American superstars. The greatest difference between the cultures lies in the way in which American fictional and dramatic genres tapped into the broad historical and cultural forces that have shaped the country. This enabled individual stars, who in any case seemed totally natural in their own right, to embody not only huge chapters of social history but also political values as real and profound as liberty and democracy. Most notoriously a second-string actor and television host named Ronald Reagan became president. However, that was less important than the fact that millions of Americans had wished that first-rate actors like Jimmy Stewart and Henry Fonda had been presidents, so fully did they seem to convey all the best American values. The historians Randy Roberts and James Olson called their substantial biography of their nation's most famous star quite simply *John Wayne: American*, whilst cultural critic Garry Wills explained that his study *John Wayne: The Politics of Celebrity* would be concerned with 'that embodied cluster of meanings and complex ideas' arising out of the actor's screen persona. The British have had a longer and less epic history than the Americans, but perhaps the time is coming when we need to explore the cultural hinterland of our leading actors. It could well be that in Wales that process is more readily undertaken.

Our actors are now very much with us, part of our everyday lives, and yet they remain a breed apart. The old ambivalence towards the strange craft of playing parts has never been fully overcome. Why is it, asked the critic W. A. Darlington, writing in the 1940s, that for all our interest in and familiarity with actors they still seem like beings 'set apart'. He wondered whether our unease with actors could be explained by the fact that they were essentially children who had not abandoned the characteristics and instincts that we all shared at an earlier age. He also suggested that another difficulty is that we are unable to draw the line between what for them is natural and what, on the other hand, is 'exhibitionism and showmanship'. One of the theatre's best-loved adages is that 'actors are often natural on stage: it is only in real life that one is unable to tell whether they are acting or not'. The fundamental questions of why there are actors and what they are about has fascinated many commentators, not least actors themselves. Our age is one in which many leading players have been readily tempted into autobiographical and professional analysis and in these musings there are familiar themes. In her splendidly titled thoughts on acting, *Other People's Shoes*, Harriet Walter succinctly sums up the way in which her job is generally perceived. She suggests that 'most societies throughout history have had a schizophrenic attitude towards the acting profession' with the consequence that 'we have been thought of as priests and as parasites, idols to be emulated and self-obsessed misfits to be scorned'. For Alec Guinness 'an actor was usually no more than an assortment of odds and ends which barely add up to a whole man'. He felt that the actor is essentially an 'interpreter of other men's words', has 'a soul which wishes to reveal itself to the world but dare not', and that he or she is 'a craftsman, a bag of tricks, a vanity bag, a cool observer of mankind, a child' and 'at best a kind of unfrocked priest who, for an hour or two, can call a heaven or hell to mesmerize a group of innocents'. Most memorably Guinness spoke of how it is that people like him hanker to be artists only to find that they are 'only an actor'. Actors have received many plaudits and honours and for some decades now American film critics have talked of individual actors as 'auteurs', as genuinely creative artists in their own right. Yet the uncertainty about the profession remains. As Walter and Guinness indicate, the old prejudices and myths now merge into modern psychological analysis.

We all readily tend to assume that there are certain personality traits that lead youngsters to take up acting. It is a profession well suited to the narcissistic, vain and extrovert but also, paradoxically, to those who are uncertain about themselves and eager to find foundations on which to build. Reading the various recent guides on acting techniques and some of the many autobiographies there are times when one wonders whether all dramatic training and acting itself are not just prolonged exercises in therapy. What Stanislavsky was after from his students was 'conscious action' in which 'energy, heated by emotion, charged with will, directed by the intellect, moves with confidence and pride'. Outsiders perceive in the training of actors an emphasis on self-understanding and self-realization that is almost unique in our educational system. Morris Carnovsky told young actors that 'you are preparing your whole psyche, your whole mind and soul, to participate in a task'. For fully trained actors there is nowhere to hide, there can be few personal myths and illusions. Of his experience of drama school Simon Callow commented that 'we all felt that if acting was not about confronting oneself in the darkest alleys of one's life, what was it?'. The whole process is one in which the attempt to achieve understanding and control can easily result in disintegration or at least vulnerability. No wonder that so many actors have reflected on the role of alcohol in the sustaining of their profession.

The Scottish actor Brian Cox willingly concedes that for many of his colleagues 'the business is an extremely painful journey'. He goes on to explain how he was weaned away from the American movies that had dominated his childhood. He took up classical British drama because of 'the richness of language' and the reward of plays 'that deal with man's struggle between his inner and outer worlds, the search for harmony, the debate of the soul'. This was a somewhat strange decision for someone who belonged to a 'working to lower middle-class' Catholic family in industrial Dundee. To become an actor he had to overcome a prejudice towards theatre which was seen as 'very much a middle-class pursuit and for people who were regarded as having a rather high opinion of themselves'. When he initially told his local youth employment officer that he wanted to act, the response was: 'Well, son, let's talk about a proper job.' Later Cox reflected that 'the need to earn a living in this manner is often undignified', and he always bore in mind the extent to which the American movie star Spencer Tracy found acting 'demeaning, cruel and embarrassing'. Richard Burton, famously, never came to terms with his chosen profession and at times admitted to being 'totally alienated' from it. According to Brian Bates, he once described it as 'the most ludicrous, undignified job in the world'. The accomplished British actor Patrick Troughton once summed up his job as 'shouting in the evening'.

All this suggests that actors, however successful, will always retain an unease about their status and role and that those societies and cultures that heap substantial praise and rewards on actors nevertheless remain a little wary of them. We seem to need them, but we do not necessarily want them in our own families or living next door. Certainly we seem to need them in our newspapers for now, more than ever, it appears that we want to know everything that is to be known about the stars of stage and screen. The line from Burbage to Burton and beyond is as concerned with mass adulation and gossip as it is with acting technique. Our need for actors has always been as much to do with their glamour and vitality as it has with their craft. Hollywood knew that there was a market for albums and magazines that was as real as that for film itself, and the gossip columns went on building on that fact to such an extent that today the fascination with showbiz and its denizens has eclipsed almost every other feature in daily newspapers. This is an international phenomenon, but perhaps to a surprising degree it is particularly characteristic of Wales where, alongside the inevitable shots and news of Madonna, Brad Pitt and George Clooney, there will be stories, however trivial, about Ioan Gruffudd, Anthony Hopkins and especially Catherine Zeta Jones. There are many dimensions to this new prominence given to Welsh actors and now, as never before, the international acclaim of Welsh talent is taken as a sign of the nation's general vitality. Almost as much as the successful rock groups, they inspire our new-found confidence. At home, we seem to need daily bulletins on their well-being; abroad, we use their names as our business card.

Where did all this new Welsh talent come from? Seemingly it came out of the blue. What a contrast with the Wales of the 1940s and 1950s when I had been enthralled first by Hollywood films and then by professional theatre, especially live Shakespeare in London and Stratford. In that development of interests play-going in Wales had played only a subsidiary part. The early experience of school pro-ductions had been followed by enthusiastic support of John Chilvers's repertory company at Swansea's Grand Theatre where amidst the farces and Agatha Christies I first experienced kitchen-sink drama, most memorably a production of *A Taste of Honey* starring Anita Morgan. Meanwhile Cardiff's New Theatre became associated with visits of star-studded London companies, my first taste being Franco Zeffirelli's production of *Romeo and Juliet*. But I took live professional theatre in Wales to be merely an occasional bonus; the real thing was going on elsewhere. Only in time did I come to realize how much the people of Wales had theatre in their bones. In all honesty I had fallen for the line that the Methodists had suppressed the interludes of Twm o'r Nant and with them the Welsh interest in drama. I had also read all those official inquiries and reports that spoke of the lack of civic amenities, and especially theatres, in urban Wales. Only later did I come to understand the extent to which the Methodists had been outmanoeuvred. Certainly there was never to be a Welsh equivalent of the West End or Broadway and there had never been a Welsh Shaw, O'Casey or Eugene O'Neill. Nevertheless, for decades countless Welsh audiences had been thrilled by great acting and subsequently inspired to take to the boards themselves.

My own interest in the Welsh experience of theatre was triggered off by a reference in Jack Jones's *Black Parade* which had been inspired by his mother's recollections of Saran, 'an illiterate brickyard girl' living in the Rhondda who became a regular theatre-goer after seeing a touring production of *Hamlet*. Subsequently, the publications of Cecil Price revealed just how many Welsh theatres had staged electrifying perform-ances by actors such as Kean, Macready, Irving, Benson and Tree. In time the Welsh responded to this entertainment by putting on plays themselves, first at the university colleges, then in the National Drama Movement, in drama competitions and in various amateur and little theatre companies. At times in the Depression it seemed as if there were more people acting in Wales than working in industry. All this enthusiasm ensured that in the post-1945 period Wales readily recruited a basic repertory company of actors to play initially in radio dramas and then later in television and the occasional film. The bridging role of radio was particularly vital. In the 1940s and 1950s, the golden age of the medium, it was radio that first brought to prominence bilingual actors such as Rachel Thomas, Gwenyth Petty, Dillwyn Owen, John Darran and Stewart Jones, who had been trained in the eisteddfod, chapel and amateur dramatic tradition of Welsh villages. There was a well-known band of Welsh actors but no sustained professional theatre. For the rest of the century professional theatre in Wales lurched from false dawn to crisis.

Meanwhile there were always pioneers calling for Welsh people, and especially their educators, to embrace drama more fully. At the 1934 National Eisteddfod Major W. P. Wheldon, permanent secretary at the Welsh Board of Education, who was presiding at the Children's Drama Competition won that year by Cwm-twrch, called for dramatics to be given a central place in the curriculum of Welsh schools. It was to take the simultaneous processes of deindustrialization and the extension of Welsh-medium education and television to create the circumstances in which Wheldon's vision could be fulfilled. Eventually, in the last twenty years of the twentieth century, the interplay between S4C and other television companies on the one hand and the new emphasis on drama in education, at school and county level, on the other allowed the Welsh to take up the challenge of enabling youngsters to prove the extent to which we are a dramatic nation. In past decades the Welsh penchant for the histrionic had been spread broadly with first the pulpit and then classrooms (not least in Essex) claiming too large a share. Now, as television and film loomed larger in Welsh life, schools could point that talent in the direction for which it was best suited. In the past we produced an occasional star together with a useful repertory company, but they had operated in a context in which dramatic opportunities in Wales were uncertain. Now, it seems, we have become more decisively a nation of actors. It is time to consider what all this means, both for the performing arts in Wales and for our culture as a whole. If we look first at the earlier stars then we will better appreciate what is exciting about the new dispensation.

# *I*vor Novello

The most appropriate starting place for a study of Welsh dramatic talent in the modern age is the National Eisteddfod held at Caernarfon in the summer of 1906. The runner-up in the soprano solo competition was somebody described in the programme simply as 'Ivor Cardiff'. This ten-year-old competitor with his big dark eyes and pale skin made a considerable impact as he delivered the Bach aria. The adjudication was made by the legendary and venerable Pencerdd Gwalia, John Thomas of Bridgend, harpist to Queen Victoria and more recently to King Edward VII. Possibly sensing that posterity or, at the very least, theatre historians awaited his judgement, old Pencerdd Gwalia told his audience that they had just 'listened to an angel singing at the throne of Grace'. That angel, masquerading as 'Ivor Cardiff', was of course, David Ivor Davies, later to become Ivor Novello, the most famous and best loved of Britain's matinée idols. At the Eisteddfod he had been billed as 'Ivor Cardiff' to disguise the fact that he was the son of Madam Clara Novello Davies, the most widely known and successful music coach in Wales. So many of her pupils had won at previous eisteddfodau that she felt that her pupils were now being discriminated against, especially in competions held away from south Wales. Anonymity had been her son's only chance.

It was entirely fitting that this young entertainer should enter history as a designated Cardiffian for he was very much a product of that seaport which would only achieve city status in 1905 when he was twelve. A case could be made for him to be regarded as Cardiff's most famous son, as much an icon of the city as Dylan Thomas has been of Swansea. In time there would be other memorials of Ivor but for some years the only indication of his roots in the city was the blue plaque placed by the television company TWW on his old home in Cowbridge Road, a thank-you to the 'Ruritanian King Who Gave His People Dreams'. I was probably one of many who looked at this plaque either from the Barry bus or from the pavement en route to Ninian Park and thought it not inappropriate that somebody with the exotic name of Novello should have been reared in this busy part of the city where Riverside merges into the shopping area of Canton. Only later did I learn that Ivor was not an exotic but very much a native and that this once smart home had been one of Cardiff's cultural centres. He was, as Peter Noble commented, of 'pure Welsh stock'; his parents had married in a Cardiff chapel and had developed their careers in the town, his handsome father David as an accountant and local government officer, his mother in the world of music.

Biographers have conceded that Ivor Novello probably owed far more to his father than has been generally assumed, not least his equable temperament and probably something of his good looks as well. But for all that, he was, as his professional name was to announce unreservedly, very much his mother's son. What was most fitting about his memorable Eisteddfod triumph was that it had been made possible and promoted by an ambitious and talented mother. The first great superstar that Wales was to offer the modern world of entertainment was classically a mam's boy. Madam Clara Novello Davies was the real McCoy, a brilliant musical facilitator, but nevertheless she belonged to a well-known Welsh type. For decades all over Wales young musicians, vocal and instrumental, were put into the hands of these larger than life, seemingly tireless and indestructible teachers who were determined to turn nervous pupils into acclaimed prize-winning artists. Much of the work went on privately in the front rooms of houses which were sometimes named 'Beethoven', often had a small bust of Bach in the window and invariably boasted a plaque outside presenting the Madam's qualifications. Parents and the wider public would come face to face with these local alchemists when they emerged to conduct their choirs or to deliver solos at important chapel services. We lived in awe of their authority, their corsets, their beauty spots and their confidence: we sensed that they were the community's only hope of distinction. It took a touch of pedigree to produce these qualities and Clara certainly had that. Doubtless much of her energy and theatricality came from an ancestor who had been a famous revivalist preacher. Her father Jacob, a good-looking former miner with a fine voice, had been much taken with the Italian singer Clara Novello whom he had heard in Cardiff and so he boldly gave his daughter a name which guaranteed a sense of identity and which subsequently confirmed the notion that artists had to take care to distinguish themselves from the general populace. In time her Welsh Ladies' Choir, triumphant in Chicago and admired by Queen

Victoria when they sang at Osborne House, became as famous as any in the world: according to the *Western Mail*'s Mario Basini its fame could be compared to that of the Vienna Boys' Choir. And all the while her Cardiff home would be visited by those musical stars who came to perform locally. Ivor met them all: he was a pageboy at the wedding of Clara Butt and he sang along with Adelina Patti. Madam Clara had set everything up for her little angel.

All over Wales students were achieving grades, winning certificates and prizes and, in so doing, giving pleasure to audiences and congregations and a deep satisfaction to their parents. The ambitions of pupils, teachers and parents varied; it was not always easy to be realistic and tears of disappointment were not unknown. Madam Clara had made it to the top in her profession and she saw no reason why her son, given all his advantages, could not do likewise. Given the degree of his exposure to Bach, Handel and Mendelssohn she had every confidence that her Ivor would be a great composer, perhaps the leading British composer of the day, a composer whose operas would be performed at Covent Garden. He was trained meticulously, first at a private academy in Cardiff and later at Oxford where between the ages of ten and sixteen he held a choral scholarship at Magdalen. He took lessons at the school and then sang with the magnificent College choir, always being given the most important solos. That wonderful opportunity ended when his voice broke but by then he was already studying composition with a Dr (later Sir) Herbert Brewer, organist at Gloucester Cathedral, where his fellow students included the future poet Ivor Gurney and composer Herbert Howells.

Musical destiny beckoned the young Ivor, but things were not to work out quite as Clara planned. She was a serious musician but she was also an entertainer, albeit in a highly respectable way. As a result, Ivor had grown up being familiar with both Bach and a broader pattern of entertainment and, whether he was in Cardiff or London, where his mother had a base, his interest and enthusiasm for popular shows was indulged. He had his own gramophone and records and, as he was appearing in various school plays, it was thought quite natural that he should be allowed to visit the theatre in both Cardiff and London. Within those theatres a whole new world was revealed and the young man was to be totally captivated by it. He was already writing his own songs and sending them off to publishers and, following his success on stage with the Cardiff Amateur Operatic Society, he was fairly certain in his own mind that he wanted to be a professional actor. Biographers have subsequently highlighted those moments when Clara, realizing what was happening, attempted to obstruct her son's plans. Nevertheless those writers stress that for all her formidable qualities she was never really in the mould of Gypsy Rose Lee's mother as depicted in the musical *Gypsy*. There was nothing grotesque in her ambitions and stratagems but over those months, as she came to terms with the inevitable, there must have been some sadness. The photographs – and in thinking of Ivor's career one is always having to go back to them – are very revealing as far as their relationship is concerned. Seen together they are obviously a team: in one shot the immaculate choirboy looks over the shoulder of a mother who seems more than a little bohemian: in another her pride in his Royal Naval Air Service uniform is all too apparent. At no stage do the photographs suggest a mother capable of effectively resisting a son's clearly expressed inclinations.

In London Ivor initially lived with his mother in Aldwych, but perhaps his future had already been shaped by two external factors. At the age of eighteen he had gone to Canada to provide the music for various imperial pageants. He was away for eleven months and, during that time, he called in on Hollywood and also spent many months in New York where he listened to and met all the great opera stars, including Caruso. More crucially, he became enchanted with the shows on Broadway. The young man had tasted independence, further experience of which was to come with the war, an event that would decisively shape his career. By the time he was conscripted into the RNAS he had already written what was to be his most famous song, one which, as Paul Webb has suggested, was so popular with military bands that abroad it was taken to be the British national anthem. 'Till The Boys Come Home', or 'Keep the Home Fires Burning' as it is more generally known, ensured that Ivor was rapidly transferred to non-combatant duties which largely involved writing popular songs for West End shows. He continued to wear his smart uniform and clearly cut a dash in theatre land. It was at this time that he met the young and well-established actor Bobbie Andrews who was to be his lifelong companion. The die was cast.

The call of empire and the challenge of war had clinched his freedom, but ultimately it was his own psychology which determined the issue and in that respect one is forced to assume that he must have been influenced by his own appearance. Throughout his childhood and adolescence his delicate skin, his soft brown eyes, his full, immaculately brushed and parted head of hair and his quiet reserved manner had all augmented his musical performances. He was the ideal choirboy and as such had matured into the perfect embodiment of the romantic military hero when the time had come to don a uniform. Such looks would surely have been wasted in any senior common room, pulpit or private study; and clearly his own predilections for the stage as well as his early success as a composer of songs would have led him to mix with precisely those people who most appreciated his beauty. His impact was best summed up by Micheál Mac Liammóir who concluded that 'his most striking quality was radiance'. The Irishman recalled that Ivor 'had merely to appear on the stage or walk into a room for that stage and that room to glow with what seemed to be the light of many lamps'. Such a luminary was obviously destined for a career in entertainment, but once again the full extent of his fame was to be determined by contemporary developments. The theatre was often able to draw on the services of very beautiful women, and we only have to look at the photographs of Gertrude Lawrence, Gladys Cooper and Lily Elsie to appreciate how high the standards were. For male actors there was a different set of requirements, at least as far as theatrical conventions were concerned. These, however, were the classic days of silent cinema and that vastly popular form of dramatic entertainment had created an enhanced demand for male beauty. Ivor Novello was eventually to achieve his real fame as a theatrical matinée idol and as a composer of stage musicals, but his initial breakthrough came as a film star and, in that respect, his remarkable appearance had been vital.

Sheridan Morley has spoken of how Ivor Novello was 'seduced into film making'. It was certainly a romantic story, one, as Geoffrey Macnab suggests, which has far more in common with those Hollywood legends of unknowns spotted serving in drugstores than is usually the case in Europe. A French director had seen a still photo of the young composer and had immediately wanted him for the part of an Englishman with Sicilian blood. It was explained that the Welshman had never acted professionally and had not been trained but the director was not deterred. Ivor first knew of this when he was cabled on the boat bringing him home from New York. He was subsequently auditioned in Paris and he went to Sicily to make *The Call of the Blood*, the first of his twenty-two films. Within a year or so of launching this new career he was, as Peter Noble argues, 'a cinema celebrity of national – indeed, one might say world renown'. A good deal has been made of Ivor Novello's film career. Most critics are of the view that he was not a great actor, but rather one whose physical beauty lent itself to the melodramatic requirements of the silent cinema. He was paid to look beautiful and to generate audience involvement as he was subjected to a variety of pressures. As Dave Berry has indicated, he was rarely to play a Britisher, certainly not a normal one. His characters, says Berry, were 'ambiguous' or 'outsiders', not infrequently 'fairly villainous or wanton, disrupting the status quo and unconstrained by society's conventional attitudes and morality'. He will be remembered most for *The Rat*, a film version of his stage hit in which he plays a Parisian apache (gigolo), and for the role of the mysterious central character in Alfred Hitchcock's *The Lodger*. He was somewhat less memorable in Hitchcock's *Downhill*, but at least in that public school story his character Roddy was allowed to recover his reputation after a false accusation of getting a girl pregnant and the film ended with him scoring a try for the Old Boys. Not many leading Welsh actors have been given the opportunity to wear rugby kit on film.

His films are not to my taste, nor is his uneven and mostly unconvincing acting. But, as is nearly always the case with silent cinema, what we remember are the looks, the poses and above all the eyes. So much is this the case that I would almost rather have the stills than see the films. It is likely that the stills were what were crucial anyway, for in silent cinema the look was everything. The look he offered was taken to be Latin: his debut in an Italian story, taken with his name, led to a general assumption of a Mediterranean background and his mother was always prepared to trot out the old Spanish Armada and the coast of Wales myth. It was an era, and film was a medium, in which one was judged by one's profile; after just a couple of movies Ivor's was declared 'perfect'. The nose was straight and just a little longer than the norm, possibly better from the right than the left. As cameramen soon realized, he looked younger straight on, more sophisticated and posher in profile. In a way his lack of formal training and perhaps even his inadequacy as an actor were less significant than the degree to which he conformed to the stereotype of a movie star. In New York he was soon hailed as 'another Valentino' and it soon became clear that he was being deliberately promoted as the British rival to the Italian star who had taken worldwide film audiences by storm when Hollywood released *The Sheik* in 1921. Sandy Wilson put things in context when he commented that Ivor's features 'embodied in one face all the romantic ideals of his age: the Latin Lover, the Sheik of Araby and the Vagabond Gypsy'. Peter Noble quotes the New York critic Paul Gallico who in 1923 found 'Mr. Novello to be as attractive as they make 'em': he 'looks a little like Conway Tearle, a little like Roman Novarro and a little like Richard Barthelmess'. This observation was perhaps very much to the point. More fundamental than the question of whether he had Latin genes was the fact that his dark, soulful and possibly dangerous looks were well suited to sustaining melodramatic suspense. In innumerable soft-focus shots he looks like the favourite son of an Italian or French family home from his training at the seminary, but there are times when his immaculate hair, white skin and broad face confirm his, albeit Celtic, Britishness. In many stills we are offered an almost mask-like face: he stares at posterity with just a hint of Keaton's chill.

Geoffrey Macnab has convincingly outlined the factors accounting for the successes and failures of Novello's cinematic career. The slightly threatening yet doleful actor with more than a touch of the adolescent appealed above all to that female audience that the movie moguls were assiduously cultivating, while his androgyny, effeminacy and rather jerky, immature movements alienated at least a section of the male audience, especially in America. He was plagued by indifferent directors, poor stories and careless casting, particularly in Hollywood where he failed to achieve the sustained employment of Llanelli's Gareth Hughes. It was to be the coming of sound, however, which finally forced him to recast his career. As nearly all the conventions of film-making were changing he took the opportunity to bring to an end the period in which he had attempted to combine work in film with live theatre. He turned to look more fully at the world which he came very quickly to see was his true home. 'I believe in the theatre' now became his heartfelt testimony.

In 1951 *The Times* obituary referred to Novello as 'a man of the theatre', explaining that he was 'one of those exceptional people' in connection with whom that phrase 'acquires meaning and virtue'. Every bit as much as his old family friend and fellow Cardiffian, Binkie Beaumont, he came to symbolize the world of West End theatre. He was one of its classic insiders who knew and loved everybody and who could judge to perfection what it was that audiences wanted to hear and see. He operated from his flat in the Aldwych and his villa at Maidenhead, he dined with all the most beautiful and charming men and women in town and meanwhile went on writing the music and producing and starring in the shows that for most theatre-goers defined the age. Starting with *Glamorous Night* in 1935 he was to write a series of musicals, often particularly associated with the Drury Lane Theatre, which were stunning successes. Occasionally he would take on a greater challenge. In 1938 he starred in a production of *Henry V* in which most critics thought him best in the quieter reflective moments. Yet again there is a sense that he did it just for the stills in which he looks incredibly kingly as he rests his chin on his gloves. It was, however, his music that people really wanted. Once again he was able to rise to the challenge of war. In 1939 he gave London *The Dancing Years* and in 1945 *Perchance to Dream* which opened with what became the song of the era, 'We'll Gather Lilacs'. As a man of the theatre he could only be compared with Noel Coward who was always both his friend and rival. As far as posterity is concerned Coward was destined to win the honours; his witty plays and songs became all the fashion and furthermore he lived on to win audiences in a new and later era. But back in the 1940s he could only envy Novello's vast public following and the affection in which he was held. They stood together as symbols of a London era, one in which they were adored by audiences and by friends and in which their private lives could be led in what was almost a club-like world. Novello was still a matinée idol, but he lived very comfortably with his friends in a distinctive subculture. As the *South Wales Echo* memorably commented at the time of his death: 'He never met the right girl.'

His work, of course, was outrageously escapist, sentimental and romantic. The words 'facile', 'superficial', 'over-sweet' and 'cloying' were often used by critics and there were occasionally further references to the inadequacy of his acting. But, as Micheál Mac Liammóir was to maintain, much of this criticism was rooted in envy and was largely beside the point. Although he was, in Philip Hope-Wallace's broadcast words, 'a master of the shameless cliché' and, according to the *Observer*'s Ivor Brown, able to offer 'tosh with a straight face and fixity of purpose', he was all the while giving audiences good theatre. His charm was always of the essence, his basic and undisputed niceness always came across and as a showman he was never less than professional. *The Times* pointed out that his strength as a writer was his 'genuine sense of "those colours that show best by candlelight"'. His last great show, *King's Rhapsody*, opened in 1949. Of Ivor's playing in the role of King Nikki of Murania, the *Evening Standard*'s Milton Shulman said that it had been done 'with all the assurance of a man who gauged public taste down to the last emotional millimetre: he never puts a wrong inflection forward nor pulls a facial muscle to no effect'.

Those facial muscles were still crucially important. He had aged but this 'Peter Pan' retained his good looks. In those final years before his early death aged fifty-eight in 1951, one of his co-stars, the Cardiff singer Olive Gilbert, said that 'even in scruffy shorts and a faded shirt he reminded one of a Greek God'. Sandy Wilson was a little harsher for he thought the body 'unremarkable': the shoulders were narrow, the chest undeveloped, the hips wide and the feet too large. 'Ivor', he reminded us, 'projected his magnetism from the neck up.' That head of his was never to let him down. If anything it became more magnificent. Famously he had declared that 'it's only my profile they like, yet every butcher boy in Naples has one twice as good'. But he was no longer putting people in mind of Italian butcher boys for, as Wilson points out, there had always been 'in the modelling of the mouth and the flare of the nostrils a dash of the Byronic aristocrat' and that was combined with something of 'the more aesthetic breed of Royalty – Ludwig of Bavaria say or Richard of Bordeaux'. Ivor was fully aware of the distinction he had acquired and he was fully justified in casting himself as a Ruritanian king. There is one amazing photograph of him in costume for *King's Rhapsody*, which adorns the cover of James Harding's biography. This is the profile in all its glory with the magnificent head set off by a silk scarf. The wide gap between his mouth and nose allows the latter to be appreciated in all its regal glory.

At the very least this personage could be a viceroy of India or even quite possibly a dowager duchess. This is the nose which had immediately caught his mother's attention when he was born: 'it's Uncle Ebenezer come back', she had declared, recalling that he had been known for having 'the largest nose in Glamorgan'.

And what of Glamorgan? The film studios in Islington and Hollywood and the West End's Drury Lane were a long way from Cowbridge Road, Cardiff. His films and music were universal but, as we have seen, Ivor Novello had moved rapidly from his mother's jurisdiction into a show-business world that was very much a closed shop and where he, always surrounded by his own entourage, was very much at home. London had become his spiritual home although he was always prepared to deepen his tan in California and the Caribbean. Paul Webb has noted how all of this led some critics to talk of how this quintessential English romantic had 'deserted his Welsh roots'. How ironic, Webb points out, that in part he was to lose his film career because, although he spoke nicely, it was none the less with a distinct Welsh accent. Welsh influences were always at hand. Madam Clara was never far away and a room was kept for her at Ivor's Berkshire home. Webb has her turning up at Ivor's great first nights 'beaming with goodwill and brandy'. She died in 1943, three years after she had published her autobiography for which her son had written a foreword. In some respects Mam had earlier been replaced by Lloydie, a Cardiffian and one of her former pupils who came out of the army in 1919 to become Ivor's secretary and, in effect, personal manager, positions he was to hold until his heart attack in 1945. Mac Liammóir reports on how splendidly Lloydie dealt with all the problems affecting the theatre, the kitchen and domestic repairs: 'it's all arranged', he would say. Within theatre circles there would be working or social sessions with other Welshmen, notably Binkie Beaumont from Cardiff's Cathedral Road and also Emlyn Williams who reserved some of his finest shafts of wit for his fellow countrymen. When he heard that Novello had gone to gaol briefly for flouting wartime petrol regulations he commented that it was a case of 'Keeping the Home Tyres Turning'.

Inevitably, there was an element of Welshness in Novello's work. Following his father's death in 1931 he wrote a play, *Proscenium*, in which he modelled the part of a middle-aged soldier on his father: in the production he played the part of that character and that of the son.

After the war he adapted his mother's autobiography as a radio play and this time he quite openly played the part of his father and himself. Biographical attention was focused on his debt to his mother but Ivor's tributes to his father revealed his awareness of how much he owed to the better looking and more stable of his parents. He did a lot of radio work: all his plays were adapted. One of the best stories to come out of Wales at that period was Cliff Gordon's *Valley of Song*. In the film it was Clifford Evans who played the part of the choirmaster whose choice of soloists for a performance of *Messiah* lead to family warfare, but on radio it was Ivor Novello who took a part for which his childhood had so fully prepared him. The evidence suggests that he might have had a hand in the way this idea had originally emerged.

The more honest and perceptive of his friends and colleagues all point to Ivor's many shortcomings. Incredibly he did not sing in public after his voice broke, he was not much of an actor and the sheer saccharine quality of his shows has guaranteed their removal from the repertoire. Advertisements suggest that his music still has a cult following but it is hardly surprising that he is now a largely forgotten figure, a mere name even to those who drink in the Ivor Davies Pub in Cardiff's Cowbridge Road. But in his lifetime the man who, for so long, looked like the son that every mother wanted and the school friend that many men yearned for just went on exuding charm and niceness. He wowed a generation and the testimony to that is formidable. Somerset Maugham's report that Churchill rather fancied Ivor has done the rounds, though opinion varies as to how far the relationship progressed. The adoration of his female fans was more openly displayed. The announcement of his death led to a degree of national mourning and huge crowds lined the streets on the day of his cremation at Golders Green. John Osborne has spoken of how his own mother, a character immortalized in his writings, felt awful that day. Commenting on how show-biz knighthoods had become almost two a penny, Osborne recalled that 'in days of yore you had to be almost dead before they handed it out: old Noel and Rattigan pined for the bauble almost into their graves'. But, he added, 'Ivor Novello, to my mother's dismay, never made it at all.' The beautiful boy from Wales, trained and groomed by a formidable and ambitious mother, had reached a certain level of achievement as he sang at Oxford and studied composition at

Gloucester. Then his charm took over and it was silent cinema and Drury Lane which gave him an enthusiastic mass constituency while at the same time theatre land allowed him the privacy to live his own life with his chosen companions. Things had worked out nicely.

# $E$mlyn Williams

If by some miracle the Wales of the mid-twentieth century had possessed a professional theatre world of its own, its own West End or Broadway, then surely Emlyn Williams would have been its chief personality. He would have been its leading impresario, its Binkie Beaumont as it were, as well as its leading playwright and actor. The man who is often referred to as 'the Welsh Noel Coward' and whom J. C. Trewin once placed in the same category as Shaw, O'Casey, Bridie and Priestley as one of 'the copious talkers of our theatre', albeit 'the most theatrically tuned and timed', was by a long chalk the most fully theatrical personality ever produced by Wales. Ivor Novello had developed a love for theatre and subsequently moved into its ambience as if joining a club or finding a comfortable new home. A later generation of actors left Wales to work on the stage or in film and yet never quite came to terms with what they were being paid to do. In contrast to Novello, Emlyn Williams was driven by an energy that made him want to transform and dominate his profession whilst, unlike other Welsh stars, he never had any doubts that he was doing not only what he did best but what he was born to do. The business of drama, the need to perform and entertain, had permeated every cell in his body. If actors are born, then this native of Flintshire used his eighty-two years of life to fulfil his destiny more completely than any other Welsh thespian.

When I first read *George*, Emlyn Williams's superb first volume of autobiography, which was published in 1961, I was struck by the story he tells about a night spent in Rouen. On a humid evening he had returned to his room in a cheap hotel to sluice himself:

> Standing in the basin, I suddenly saw with a start, three yards away, a naked male figure, one leg bent, one thigh turned towards me, eyes fiercely on mine, as if to say 'Eh Bien?'. By the light of the one candle, sunburnt face against the cave-dark background, he looked except for the whiteness of his body like one of those sullen strapping shepherds in Italian paintings. I stared back, boldly; in the first long mirror I had ever been alone with, I was studying myself. 'Eh Bien', I said aloud, 'you're going out tonight!'

And out he went for a memorable evening which represented yet another significant step in the process by which this Oxford undergraduate developed a love of France and an ever fuller appreciation of both the company and physical beauty of young men and women. *George* created quite a stir at the time and it remains one of the most sensitive and honest accounts of physical awakening, in particular revealing as it does the essential narcissism of its author. Not all actors are narcissists, but all actors have to come to terms with full-length mirrors and it does help if one is a little bit in love with what they show. Unlike Novello, Emlyn Williams was not blessed with the looks of a god but he never gave anything less than an impression of being very satisfied with what he had to offer. He was totally at ease with his looks and used them to maximum effect. To me he was essentially feline and he exuded all the satisfaction that most cats express as they tidy up their bodies after a delicious snack. It was no accident that 'George' Williams was preening himself when he first saw the man who was in the process of becoming Emlyn in that Rouen mirror. Surely the basic drive behind all successful acting comes from learning the particularly personal lesson taught by the mirror, maximizing that lesson and then offering it publicly to the masses.

*George* made its impact largely because its readers could relate to the way in which its hero, Emlyn's earlier self, discovered the successive joys of boyhood and adolescence. It quite beautifully traces the way in which a youngster living in the early twentieth century developed the love of an infinitely more exciting second language, comics, magazines, books, school, the cinema, theatre and finally, as we have seen, France and sex. Of those who have written about their discovery of entertainment in Wales perhaps only the novelist Jack Jones tackled it with the same sense of excitement as Emlyn Williams. He writes magically on the process of how 'the Pictures' came to dominate his life and of how initially he had been 'captured' by the serials. Even more memorable, however, is his explanation of how 'the marshmallow of the films became judiciously mixed with the more staple diet of school'. Meanwhile, live theatre had not made anything like the same impact. His mother had taken him to see a play about 'village-folk' performed by an amateur group from Ffynnongroyw. The trouble was that the play was performed in Welsh, the everyday language of the hearth and chapel, and therefore 'as dull as real life'. His mother had been more impressed: she had liked the live sparks which had emanated from a real anvil, and had thought the blacksmith 'had a look of those Protheroes that worked with your father's cousin'.

But then came a trip to the Royalty Theatre in Chester to see *Dick Whittington*. The amateurs of Ffynnongroyw were easily eclipsed, as indeed was the far more potent and hitherto relished Hippodrome Cinema in Connah's Quay. The pantomime itself was nothing, no threat to 'the magic of the Pictures', but the theatre itself had been a revelation. 'The Williams's', he reported, 'had been swallowed up into the great family Gallery' and he personally had been put under a spell: 'the steady clamour', 'the smell of dust and soap and gas-jets', the overture and the curtain rising all enraptured the child. That child was soon reciting regularly in the eisteddfodau held at Holywell County School as well as experimenting with writing and acting. The training and exercises, however, were less important than the impact of the outside world. On his way to France he had to pass through London. From his taxi he saw for the first time 'Shaftesbury Avenue, a flashing farrago of names, Moscovitch The Great Lover Queen's Nightie Night Evelyn Laye Globe Her Husband's Wife Marie Luhr, limitless noise, movement, buildings, crowds, red bus after red bus streamed into the names of plays, His Majesty's Chu Chin Chow Fifth Year—'. He was, of course seeing the future. He still had to experience the pain and pleasure of Oxford and his liberation by the Oxford University Dramatic Society, but more than anything else he had discovered where he 'belonged'. He had been 'overwhelmed', just 'like a toddler swept up by a mammoth of a mother and folded to a gargantuan bosom'. Inevitably, on that first night in London, he had seen a show: from his hotel he took to the streets and very soon he was in the gallery listening to the orchestra tune up at the Victoria Palace Theatre.

Like Novello, Emlyn Williams received no formal training. Having become a student actor at Oxford he suffered a breakdown and took more fully to writing as part of his recovery. In 1927 his play *Full Moon* was put on at the Oxford Playhouse and a little later he made his professional debut as an actor on the London stage. In that same year he made his Broadway debut and then in 1928 his play *Glamour*, a story of Welsh actors in London, opened at the Embassy in London before transferring to the Royal Court. In this process of becoming a man of the theatre it is fascinating to trace the steps whereby he discovered his niche. Richard Findlater has highlighted his 1930 role in Edgar Wallace's *On the Spot*, in which he played the faithful henchman Angelo to Charles Laughton's Chicago-Italian racketeer. It was as Angelo, argues Findlater, that Emlyn Williams first displayed 'that mixture of macabre sweetness and gentle terrorism which has made at least one of his reputations'. Later that year London audiences and critics alike were being terrified by his own play *A Murder Has Been Arranged* in which the author not only presented a murder and a ghost but also a full character analysis of the criminal. Emlyn had disclosed what was to be a lifelong interest in gruesome murder. That interest resulted most famously in his 1935 play *Night Must Fall*, a tale of a charming baby-faced, cruel young man who kills women, in which he starred first in London and New York and then almost everywhere. This play, described by Findlater as 'a minor classic of the macabre', became a repertory standard and was twice filmed. Thirty-two years later he was to publish *Beyond Belief*, the product of his total fascination with the Moors murderers.

It is a matter of great regret that Emlyn Williams is not available to offer himself as a subject for radio's *In the Psychiatrist's Chair*. Did the preening before the mirror reveal the savagery that is in the nature of every cat, or was it just that the tendency to cast the Welshman as an exotic of one sort or another tempted him to develop the menace that his slightly affected and insidious Welsh accent suggested? Above all, of course, he had wanted to make an impact; certainly, as James Harding argues, he brought 'a nouveau frisson' to the professional stage. In all his parts, whether macabre or not, he had edge – an attribute on which he could cash in even as he played to his own strengths. In this respect Harding very tellingly quotes Sir John Gielgud who always felt that Emlyn Williams's 'narrative talent had something of the Welsh streak about it': in particular there was 'a kind of story-in-the-dorm schoolboy gift which he could employ with great invention and freedom but which could not bear too close investigation'. This is a marvellous observation and takes us back to the young George growing up in the pub at Glanrafon listening to the miners speaking in Welsh and visitors telling stories in a strange tongue. Findlater's wonderfully perceptive speculation on the early days of the first 'working-class writer of any size in English dramatic writing since Ben Jonson' prompts an interpretation of Emlyn Williams's career as one in which he wanted events on stage to be as vivid as those early stories heard in the bar or read in comics. Biographers have stressed the truly Cinderella aspects of his career; certainly there can be no other in which the candlelight and shadows of the home were transformed so dramatically into the artificial intensity of the theatre world. J. C. Trewin once made the shrewd observation that it is far more difficult for the playwright to sustain metaphysical suspense than it is for the writer of prose: 'ghoulies and ghosties' are bound to be uneasy companions on the stage. Citing his play *Trespass*, which involved attempts to communicate with the dead in a remote north Wales castle, Trewin referred to the dramatist's gift of 'making the naked heart knock at the ribs in that crackle of atmospherics'.

'Atmospherics' were to be his hallmark and that in many ways was what *George* had been all about. The term 'Gothic' was to be applied to *Trespass* as with much else of his work and in *George* we witness the impressionable child responding to the gothic in the Bible and its related stories, in comics and in popular culture generally. That child was later in life to be especially associated with the works of Charles Dickens. In *George* we are shown why that was to be the case. It is a book that evokes a thoroughly Dickensian world. In a variety of prose forms Dickens had brought together many aspects of the Victorian imagination. Notions of good, evil, character, happiness and danger were, in particular, to have an enormous impact on the popular culture of the era that followed his death. In *George* we see the young lad responding to tales told by Dickens, initially courtesy of magazines and books and then at performances by John Duxbury, an itinerant elocutionist. More memorably we are told of George's first experience of the films of D. W. Griffith, the Hollywood director whose work was rooted in Dickens, as indeed was so much of silent cinema. In his autobiography Emlyn Williams testified to the impact of Dickens on his generation, and in his professional career he was to sustain that influence to a greater extent than any of his contemporary colleagues in either theatre or cinema.

That menacing and melodramatic edge that would characterize his dramatic work was dictated by his psychological and physical characteristics and honed by his education in the gothic. Those qualities that were to shape his memorable theatrical villains such as Shakespeare's

Angelo, Richard III, Shylock and Iago were very evident in his busy schedule of film work on the eve of the Second World War. It was a time when British cinema was desperately attempting to catch up with Hollywood's ability to tell stories of ordinary people in realistic settings, a departure made urgent by the inevitable approach of what was bound to be a people's war. New kinds of stories and new kinds of acting were badly needed and as films dealing with working-class people in industrial and regional settings went into production there were bound to be openings for an established Welsh actor from a humble background. In what was to be a new chapter of British realist cinema Emlyn Williams was to make his mark, but he did so playing villains who, effective as they were, owed more to the conventions of melodrama than to the strict demands of verismo. He always injected into his work an added dimension that was in part theatrical but also (and it was this that made him truly memorable) in part psychological. It was perhaps his own interest in the psychopathic roots of evil which enabled him to invest his characters with that kind of motivation. There was always the risk of his going too far, especially as the voice was so distinctive, but at his best his villainy was geared to the demands of the story.

Three of Williams's screen characters of that era are best summed up as 'ferrety', to use Dave Berry's description. In *The Citadel*, the 1938 film of A. J. Cronin's story in which an idealistic young doctor has to come to terms with the realities of life first in the Valleys of south Wales and then in London, he played the local miners' leader who essentially ran the Medical Aid Society as a scam. In true Hollywood style MGM were far more interested in the trials and tribulations of the hero than in the wider social issues and they adhered closely to the convention that a trade union was above all a restricted practice. This suited Emlyn, who could relish his racket and outmanoeuvre the innocent newcomer. That same year he starred in an excellent and very important British thriller, *They Drive by Night*, in which a wrongly accused murder suspect takes refuge in the world of lorry drivers. His character is innocent of any crime but, nevertheless, this Welshman is on the run and resents the way he is being pursued. What was called for was a sustained depiction of tension and frustration on the part of a little man living on the edge of an underworld. Emlyn delivered in full. Rather more attention was given to a bigger and more expensive production released early in the war and again based on a Cronin novel. *The Stars Look Down* was a vehicle for Michael Redgrave who played a young miner who receives a college education and who, resisting various temptations, accepts that his destiny is to go back to lead the miners of his village in their fight against ruthless employers and for nationalization. The story is set in the Durham coalfield but the Americans always described this as a film about Wales, although the only Welsh element in it is provided by Emlyn's character Joe Gowlan. In the film, Gowlan is a contemporary of the Redgrave hero Davy Fenwick and like him is a miner's son who himself works in the pit. As things unfold Davy becomes a teacher and then a defender of the miners whilst all the while Joe milks every opportunity of making money and achieving the good things in life. He is a chiseller, a classic Hollywood villain attuned to every opportunity that the city and commerce have to offer and quite prepared to betray family and friends in the process. The character is totally evil but, in responding to this opportunity of exploiting what he did best, Emlyn Williams steals the film, not least because Redgrave is so deadly earnest. Ultimately, his villainy is over the top and melodramatic but, earlier, the charm of this trilby-wearing bow-tied opportunist can be seen as an understandable response to the challenge of getting out of the pit village and into the mainstream. It took many different types of energy to escape the remorseless logic of the Depression and one feels initially that Emlyn's Joe was just cashing in on what chances there were. Before the melodrama takes over one senses that the charm and energy on display here were very much those of the actor himself.

The vitality of his characters ensured that Emlyn Williams could never be accused of dealing in stereotypes. The extent to which they were defined and motivated by his understanding of their psychology meant that the actor never had to worry about his Welshness. J. C. Trewin reminds us that until that time 'the Welshman, if he appeared at all on the English stage, was presented only as a comic Taffy or an ignorant provincial, a butt or a boor'. By creating characters who existed in their own right Emlyn Williams had given notice to that era in theatre history, but even more importantly he was to do the same thing as far as his writing was concerned. Trewin argued that Emlyn had paved the way for a new generation of Welsh actors: he had been 'an interpreter of Welsh life in the theatre'. Above all in this respect he had written *The Corn is Green*, the play which first opened in London in 1938 and New York in 1940 and which was to become a classic of the modern repertoire as well as being filmed twice for the cinema and twice for television. The story is set in 'Glansarno, a small village in a remote Welsh countryside' and the action opens in the book-lined living room of an old Welsh house as a character called John Groney Jones, 'a shabby Welshman of forty', sings 'Pechadur wyf, y dua'n fyw'. Wales had truly come to the West End and was being presented to the world as never before. Naturally, the playwright milks what could have been thought of as an alien setting for all its worth and there were elements of comic relief but, as Trewin and other critics note, the setting is used legitimately and intelligently and in every respect buttresses the authenticity of the story. The story of the dedicated teacher discovering that a pitboy has the potential to be a genius obviously had a universal appeal, but from the outset audiences and critics appreciated that the Welsh dimension was particularly appropriate. The otherness of Welsh life and the second-language factor, taken with the culture's known reverence for the printed word and education generally, all contributed to a deepening of the relationship between teacher and pupil.

Although Emlyn played the part of the pitboy Morgan Evans in the original production and the British public were well aware of how important his own teacher Miss Cooke had been in his life (there is a marvellous photograph taken at the christening of his son Alan in which Miss Cooke in fashionable hat stands alongside Alan's godfather Noel Coward who in his trilby hat looks for all the world like a bookie), it was only with the publication of *George* that we realized how fully auto-biographical the play had been. It was a play that was taken up by the theatre worldwide but its resonances were always particularly significant in Wales, for the story was one which specifically highlighted a classic Welsh relationship. The joys and tensions of the original George–Miss Cooke pairing, then of the fictional Morgan–Miss Moffat, were to be replicated on countless occasions in Wales as talents, scholarly, scientific, musical, dramatic or sporting, were identified in classrooms throughout the country. To a greater extent than in any comparable culture successful Welsh men and women were to identify the teachers who had set them on their way. What clinches the authenticity of Emlyn Williams's story is its emphasis on the possibilities of betrayal and jealousy. The relationship operated on several levels, and there were many temptations on the path to the grail of success. At every twist and turn there were drinking mates or seductive partners to lure the young man away from the straight and narrow and there were other tensions too. In *George* there is a marvellous moment when Miss Cooke intervenes to tug at her student's robe just as, in the part of Shylock, he was threatening Gratiano with a knife. Young George was furious at her destruction of the scene: was she, he later speculated, deliberately 'pricking the bubble' of his ambition?

To look at the original 1938 cast list of *The Corn* is to appreciate how much Emlyn Williams did for the Welsh acting profession. The first Miss Moffat was Dame Sybil Thorndike but she and Emlyn were surrounded by Welsh talent, as he was to be in many of his ventures. It is no exaggeration to say that he himself was something of a Miss Moffat for a generation of Welsh actors, for he opened up all kinds of possibilities. In 1944 his play *The Druid's Rest* opened in London. This was another chapter of autobiography, dealing this time with a younger Welsh child whose education develops in 'the back-parlour of a small public-house in the Welsh village of Tan-y-Maes'. The part of the publican was played by Roddy Hughes, a Welsh actor who was a great friend of Emlyn; his eldest son Glan, whose first words in the play, 'Yn y spench, 'nhad dan y paraffin', were spoken in answer to his father's question, was played by the young Richard Burton who was making his London debut. Burton had been chosen for the part after an audition held at Cardiff's Sandringham Hotel. Famously, when Miss Cooke first saw this latest Welsh schoolboy wonder she told Emlyn, 'he's like you but he has the devil in him'. That devil was seen in part when Burton, in the company of his understudy Stanley Baker, went in search of wine, women and song as the show toured in Wales and elsewhere. As Burton's career was nurtured by Emlyn Williams the question of raising his salary arose: he was sent to see Binkie Beaumont who told the young actor that he supposed that he had been put up to it by 'that old Welsh pit pony'. Emlyn, comments James Harding, loved that.

That Emlyn Williams was playing midwife to a new era was again apparent in 1949 with the release of *The Last Days of Dolwyn*, a film which he wrote and directed. As Dave Berry has effectively argued we can only regard this movie as a lost opportunity. Emlyn was altogether too concerned with dark gothic atmosphere and with creating a romantic pastoral 'once upon a time' type of community to worry much about any real political issues. The flooding of a Welsh valley is treated melodramatically without any of the contemporary allusions which even the Ealing comedies of the day managed to fit in. Nevertheless, here was a Welsh director who, having already toured his West End play about Wales in the principality, was now setting up a Welsh film that further proved that there was available a repertory company of native actors capable of sustaining an indigenous cinema. The cast was bristling with possibilities: Emlyn Williams himself played the excessively malicious villain and alongside him was a smouldering Richard Burton making his film debut. Roddy Hughes was once again a publican and, best of all perhaps, Hugh Griffith dominated the village as its sombre minister. One can almost sense Burton and Griffith, in particular, yearning for stronger material and for fuller opportunities. Nevertheless, the whole exercise provides a significant clue to the nature of Emlyn Williams's art. Having taken so much care to find the right locations in Wales, to design the right kind of village and to ensure atmospheric lighting, special effects and photography, he failed to control the writing. For him atmosphere and melodrama were more important than narrative, let alone social analysis. His biggest mistake was his own character, for he could never be content with a mere political situation such as the English suppressing the Welsh or the gentry cheating the peasants. This valley is to be flooded merely because Rob Davies was long ago driven out for pilfering chapel money and has now returned to get his revenge. One almost feels that given half a chance he would be sawing people in half or tying maidens to railway lines. As Findlater commented, 'Williams the artist was betrayed by Williams the entertainer'. He was still in the world of comic book entertainment.

It was altogether appropriate that Emlyn Williams was to achieve his greatest fame and certainly his fullest accolades by returning to that world in which his young imagination had first been fired. He had felt his 'spine tingle' when as a schoolboy he had read his first Dickens story and understood for the first time 'that the magic mind out of the *Companion* and the Pictures (the cinema) could also be found in a classic'. Having listened to John Duxbury, the elocutionist, he had taken to giving chapel recitations himself and one of his pieces had been 'Mr Sergeant Buzfuz' from *Pickwick Papers*. His first professional Dickens reading however did not come until 1951: the idea had come to him as he read *Bleak House* to his young sons and then over a two-year period he had been carefully selecting material. Recent biographers of Dickens have emphasized how much the great novelist enjoyed reading his own material to audiences, and they have linked this to his own fascination with live entertainment, especially theatre, and with his own love of performing. We are reminded that the man who was to be popularly associated with the morality and respectability of the Victorian family was in reality always something of a Regency dandy. Very quickly, Emlyn Williams saw that he could perfectly embody all the vanity, melodrama and sentimentality that had been the essence of Dickens's own public persona. Dickens had died in 1870 aged only fifty-eight: Williams began his public life as Dickens in 1951 when he was forty-six and was still performing the part in the 1980s when he was in his eighties. He had long outlived his mentor, but for all those years his presentation of the master was utterly authentic. I saw him twice as Dickens: there was a twenty-five year gap between the performances but little had changed. We were taken back to the Victorian candlelit era of shadows and made aware of the original power of the tales. Everything was meticulous; the actor was bringing the novelist alive and somehow it was always the peeling off of the white gloves which clinched the illusion. G. K. Chesterton once provided a wonderful prose evocation of Dickens the man, and essentially he was describing Emlyn as well. The novelist had given the impression of being small, he was 'pale of visage', he had a large and mobile actor's mouth, 'exceptionally bright and active eyes', a generally 'flashy' or 'Frenchified appearance' and a delicate and even 'effeminate' facial profile. In his readings the use of the eyes had been vital. That was very much the case with Emlyn Williams too. It was always the eyes that did most to sustain the tension.

Emlyn Williams never met Dylan Thomas and indeed did not know of his verse until he heard the young Richard Burton reciting it. After Thomas's death, however, he took to performing the poet's writings. In contrast to his Dickens act, he did not attempt to act out the part but rather just stepped forward as himself to perform Dylan and especially his prose writings. They had a few things in common: Dylan's voice was posher but they both relied on an exaggerated and fanciful declaiming to achieve effect. They had also both been impressionable youngsters who had never lost a fascination with the sounds, shadows, follies and foibles that surround an infant in an adult world. It was Emlyn Williams's good fortune that as a young man he had discovered that the theatre was a world in which he could indulge in the sensations that had always thrilled him as a child. When his playwriting days were done it was the personas of Dickens and Dylan which allowed him to maintain his theatrical roots. Courtesy of those two notable authorities on childhood, he was able to keep alive the world of George.

# *R*ichard Burton

The story of how the Port Talbot schoolteacher Philip Burton first taught and then tutored, fostered and renamed the teenager Richard Jenkins who went on to achieve fame as an actor and then notoriety as a lover, boozer and conspicuous spender is as melodramatic and as frequently told as any fiction devised by a Welsh writer. It is a wonderful story, not least because of the way it feeds off and appeals to so many aspects of the Welsh psyche. With it we are back in the world of Emlyn Williams's Miss Moffatt with, once again, a teacher operating as alchemist. Remarkably *The Corn is Green* was first being staged just as Philip Burton was producing gold in Port Talbot. And yet no novelist or dramatist would have risked allowing their fictional pupil to achieve either the critical or financial success which the real-life Richard Burton would go on to achieve. To thrill the English theatrical establishment with performances of Hal, Hamlet and Coriolanus was one thing, but then to move on to a breathtaking life of glamour involving the world's most beautiful woman and most expensive diamond was another. The story's anticlimactic ending was perhaps more predictable. Our Calvinism would lead us to expect a cautionary tale, our Celtic romanticism would have prepared us for the fact that our hero was either too innocent or too inflexible to come to terms with the prosaic realities of an alien culture.

The Richard Burton story has often been told and necessarily our response remains ambivalent. We take enormous pride in his achievement of taking London by storm and we allow ourselves a wry smile as we think of his sheer chutzpah in walking off with the world's most beautiful and famous woman and thinking that he could get away with it. At the same time we feel a collective guilt that things went awry, that his drinking and subsequent physical decline were so publicly exposed in a series of poor films and in the widely reported absurdities of the soap opera that his love life became. The thought that someone in England might say 'what else would you expect from a Welshman' really hurts.

Our frequent telling of the story has to do with dimensions other than melodrama for, unlike Ivor Novello and Emlyn Williams, the young Richard Jenkins had embarked on a career in which many possibilities suggested themselves. His two predecessors had been psychologically, emotionally and sexually predisposed to be men of the theatre. In rather different ways they both appreciated the safe refuge offered by the conventions and friendship of the theatre. They were both able to be themselves whilst all the while remaining confident that a firm line could be drawn between what they did in costume and their private lives. It was because they were so clearly 'actorly' that allowances could be made for them. They were naturals, licensed to entertain and licensed too to be different in the way theatre folk are, whether in London or living and working in small towns. In contrast, the whole point about the young man who became Richard Burton was that, quite apart from being brilliant on stage, he was essentially a product of a community; he was one of us. It is that tantalizing fact, far more than the familiar details of his decline, which keeps him so firmly in our minds. We are reluctant to let our memory of him fade because several issues frustratingly remain unresolved.

As is generally appreciated, and it is a point to which we must return, Burton was always somewhat ashamed of being an actor. An essential aspect of his decline was his failure to take his profession seriously. At the same time, he was never anything less than proud of the bilingual culture of the Valleys of south Wales and he saw himself as an unmistakable product of them. He identified with that largely Non-conformist culture, often confessing that if he had been born a decade or so earlier he would have been declaiming from a pulpit. He supported its rugby teams and would have given anything to have achieved the distinction of his contemporaries Bleddyn Williams and Cliff Morgan. Of course he treasured literature, building up his own library and learning chunks of verse quite independently of lines that had to be learnt professionally. But he very much resented not being a writer himself. He tried his hand at essays and stories, all the while wishing that he could write like Gwyn Thomas or the young Dylan. Politically, too, he identified with Wales and an important part of him wished that he could use his voice to dominate the House of Commons in the manner of his hero Aneurin Bevan. Now this kind of Walter Mitty-like identification with the most obviously vibrant and successful strands of a culture is a syndrome which was indulged in by many young south Walians as they made their way through grammar school, but the point with Burton is that there was always the sense that he might have been capable of fulfilment in any of these directions. We are left with a double frustration. Was it just a mischance that allowed Philip Burton to put his ward on the stage? With a different mentor would the pupil have gone on to be a sportsman, a writer or politician? And if the actor had within him those possibilities, how annoying it is that as an actor he was seldom if ever afforded the opportunity to play characters who were involved in stories relating to contemporary Welsh affairs. If he could not be our greatest novelist or prime minister, he should at least have played the parts. It is in these respects that his personal failure to fulfil his promise was a failure which not only affected our culture but was very much part of it.

In 1989 I spent an afternoon with Philip Burton sipping sherry at his home in Key West. As we reflected on the ups and downs of his foster son's career I realized that the man with whom I was talking was far more a man of the theatre than Richard Burton had ever been. What is more, Philip Burton's lifelong interest and involvement in theatre had developed very naturally in his native south Wales. In his 1969 auto-biography *Early Doors*, which he appropriately subtitled 'My Life and the Theatre', Burton described how important live entertainment had been in the mining community of Mountain Ash where he was born in 1904. In the town's two theatres he enjoyed grand opera, Shakespeare and Gilbert and Sullivan as well as a local repertory company, and his own career as an actor started courtesy of the YMCA. In Cardiff, where as an undergraduate he studied maths and history, he visited the three theatres and recalled with particular pleasure the performance of Sir John Martin-Harvey who in his younger days had learnt his trade with Sir Henry Irving. In 1925 (as it happens the year of Richard Jenkins's birth) Philip Burton became a schoolmaster at Port Talbot and it was at the secondary school, and more especially the YMCA in that town, that his career as an actor, director and author of plays really took off. Whatever the degree of his previous interest in theatre it is very apparent that it was at Port Talbot that Burton became caught up in what was a local passion. He commented how 'during those years in Wales there was a great outburst of dramatic activity' and highlighted the way in which local societies, such as his at the YMCA, competed fiercely in professionally adjudicated drama festivals. Undoubtedly, it was the passion and intensity of this competitive theatre which honed his skills and which led not only to his winning prizes as an actor and director but also to his writing plays which were to be widely performed by the various clubs. From this there followed his work as a drama lecturer and part-time BBC producer. No other contemporary career so well illustrates the extent to which theatre was an integral part of everyday life in Welsh industrial communities in the Depression years. Interestingly, Philip Burton was to note that 'the leading members of most of the dramatic societies in Wales were teachers'.

We can imagine that there were teachers in classrooms all over Wales inculcating skills and then subsequently in drama clubs attempting to induce a wider cultural fulfilment in much the same way as their colleagues would be doing with young musicians and footballers. In this extramural tuition there must inevitably have been elements of subjectivity. In Philip Burton's case there was his understandable passion for Shakespeare. Apparently, for he claimed no memory of the incident, it was whilst setting up a Shakespeare pageant that he first encountered a Richard Jenkins whom he was to reject at first audition. But there were additional interests and values that this particular teacher brought to his lessons and rehearsals. Although a native of south Wales, Philip Burton was the son of English parents and he had been brought up as an English-speaking, music-loving youngster who found particular satisfaction and fulfilment in the language and music of the Anglican Church, or the Church in Wales as it became in 1920. Subsequently, at the commencement of the Second World War and just as his links with the BBC were developing, Burton found himself a flight lieutenant in charge of the 499 Squadron of the Air Training Corps. In other words, as the young Richard Jenkins began to move into the sphere of influence of his local drama instructor he must have been very aware of a whole new set of conventions and values that were on offer. In a remarkable process of transition the adolescent moved from the Welsh-speaking home of a coal miner into the lodgings of a schoolteacher whose consuming passions centred on those institutions which essentially defined the most respected aspects of Englishness. As he switched both his home and his name, the young Richard was being given the opportunity to claim a place in an English-language culture that was very different from the one that prevailed on the streets of Port Talbot.

In the stage directions of his play *Granton Street* Philip Burton stressed that his south Wales family were to speak in accents 'far removed from that offstage Welshman' and that there should be 'no exaggerated rolling of r's and hissing of s's'; they were to speak 'just plain English'. Later he admitted that there were 'some beautiful Welsh accents', but added the explanation that they 'don't belong to the industrial towns'. He was always at pains to stress that Richard Jenkins had come to him wanting to be an actor, even at one stage suggesting that the youngster had picked him out as someone who was likely to take over his life. Nevertheless, whatever the forces that brought them together, the teacher had no doubts concerning his first priority, for 'to begin with, Richard had to get rid of an ugly Welsh accent'. This was no easy matter for 'his rough industrial Welsh dialect was a major obstacle'. Burton then explained that 'it took almost two years of gruelling work to get rid of it' and then in what sounds entirely like an admission of guilt he revealed that this task was 'infuriating' for sometimes 'in the middle of a lively conversation, the pedagogical devil in me would pounce upon a wrong vowel sound'. The process, one suspects, was not without tears.

It was Philip Burton's destiny as a man of the theatre to manufacture one of the great actors of the English-speaking world. There were other aspects to his career: an earlier pupil, Owen Jones, had gone to RADA and the Old Vic only to die in the wartime RAF, and Burton himself went on to an honourable career first with the BBC and then as a drama instructor in New York. But these achievements were as nothing compared with his role in the production of the man who would become world-famous as Richard Burton. Clearly, we must identify the actor's spectacular career as having its true roots in that ferment of dramatic activity in the 1930s: one can well appreciate a talented youngster responding to the local thespians as being the liveliest aspect of a dull depressed town. The romantic in the young Jenkins had drawn him to music and verse and then he had passed into the hands of an instructor who gave him a voice that would allow some kind of success in English professional life. But there was more to acting than this: what was needed above all was some kind of stage presence and in this respect the early reactions to Richard Burton were fascinating.

In the West End Olivier's brilliance had created a new expectation.

Post-war audiences wanted to be physically thrilled. These were the years when the critic Kenneth Tynan had identified Olivier's 'panther like' qualities and related that dimension in his acting to the great tradition of Garrick, Kean and Irving. In the theatre there had to be something more than elegance, mannerisms and good diction. Collectively, the English theatre-going public were keen to spot 'Olivier's heirs'. One possibility was Paul Scofield whose 1948 Hamlet at Stratford had been described as 'an animal that prowled'. The scene was set for Burton, although it was apparent that in some respects he was greatly disadvantaged. Throughout the period of his initial successes in London and Stratford critics would draw attention to his physical handicaps: even Binkie Beaumont, who was to organize his London debut, referred to his 'thick and clumsy body' and thereafter there were to be constant references to his 'stockiness' and lack of heroic stature. More predictably critics vied with each other in attempts to come up with an appropriate class or sporting tag: was he a kind of 'boxer-poet', a 'rugby-playing Hamlet', or a prince with 'coal-miner's legs'? Even T. C. Worsley, who liked his Hamlet, argued that Burton had none of the right qualities for the part for 'he cannot suggest the poet, nor the courtier, nor the scholar'. In general, critics found his mature Henry V, in which some sense of stature was needed, far less impressive than his young Prince Hal, and in comic roles he impressed nobody. More surprisingly, given his later reputation, there were initially many derogatory comments on his speaking voice. There were references to its hardness, shrillness, inaudibility and monotony, especially in the upper register. Tynan thought that there was an element of 'rant' in his Henry and there were more general references to a lack of poetry and irony in the voice. The critic of *The Times* pointed to a sullenness and melancholy in his acting whilst the novelist Caryl Brahms thought his presence not sufficiently 'sunny'; rather he had a 'strange curdled quality'.

These early negative responses are worth noting, not least because they discredit the notion that a brilliant beginning gave way in Burton's career to a fall from grace; in fact, his acting was never as flawless as the legend suggests. But they serve also to underline how incredible his initial impact was for, even with these shortcomings, these departures from West End norms, the young Welshman who was clearly an outsider nevertheless impressed the critics and even more noticeably thrilled the paying customers. There was something about him; he had what Beaumont called 'sheer star magnetism'. Famously, in his first important West End role he had invested Christopher Fry's verse drama *The Lady's Not for Burning* with precisely the spiritual quality for which the author had been looking. Time and time again, as Philip Hope-Wallace explained, 'the eye picks him out and refuses to leave him'. Here in a play that in part was concerned with the building of a church he was, in the words of Harold Hobson, 'a young knight keeping a long vigil in the cathedral of his own mind'. In his subsequent Shakespearean roles his charm, stillness and spiritual quality were always the foundation of his performance. His head, said Alec Guinness, was that of a Roman emperor, and Anthony Quayle spoke of him as having 'the heaven-sent actor's mask' with wide-apart eyes and good cheek bones. The high water mark of his stage career came at the Old Vic in the early 1950s when the thirty-year-old Burton gave a new young generation of theatre-goers a range of Shakespeare performances that spoke to them directly. By now there was a natural authority and confidence in his voice and movement, and yet it was felt that this young actor was very much of his time, a product of a new post-national service meritocratic and democratic culture in which miners' sons could indeed play kings and princes.

In 1991 I wrote a short book on Richard Burton which I subtitled 'So Much, So Little', a phrase I adapted from a Binkie Beaumont judgement on his protégé. The book reflected my own disappointment with the way that Burton's career developed but also advanced the argument that the actor had been unlucky in his failure to find a milieu in which he could sustain his professional career with any degree of cultural and emotional satisfaction. All those critics not susceptible to the Burton charm had found it easy enough to point to the way in which he had set about digging his own early grave. He clearly wanted fame and fortune and loved taking every dollar Hollywood offered as well as the new-found opportunity to fall in love with the world's most beautiful women. His drinking was always an important part of his identity and several of his colleagues told me that he was always at his best in the pub, where he could indulge in his preferred roll of raconteur and conversational performer. Later, his drinking became a matter of assuaging personal and professional guilt. Perhaps there was never any hope of his being rescued but it is difficult not to wonder whether things might have been different had he fallen in with the right authors and directors. It seemed to me as if he was forever just missing a boat. He never felt at home in Binkie Beaumont's world of theatre gays and luvvies – a world in part later sustained by Lawrence Olivier – and he had already left for Hollywood by the time that the new post-Osborne era opened. In Hollywood, too, it was an era of transition and ultimately it seems that his film career was just a matter of pot-luck. And, as he was so often to complain, there was as yet no real film or theatre structure in Wales to which he could relate. As I wrote my book I found myself wishing for just that moment of fortune which would have brought him together with a great writer or director who could have guided him in the right direction. A decade on I would want to reiterate this point, and I remain convinced that the 1960s were a bad time for a classic English/Welsh actor rapidly approaching middle age. The flaw in this argument, however, is obvious, for every actor has to make his own luck and the sad truth is that Richard Burton never really attempted to mould his own artistic destiny. Nor at any stage did he attempt to define what he was best at doing or take steps to recruit the talent to ensure that he was accepting the work and roles that would allow him to generate genuine theatrical or cinematic excitement. There was, then, a huge artistic failure at the core of his career. There was a failure of nerve as well. The usual explanation of this passivity is his contempt for the acting profession: his job, says Melvyn Bragg, was for him a huge 'cosmic joke'. And so it was that a drunken Burton would do his Broadway Hamlet in different accents on different nights according to whim or who was in the audience: one night he did his 'To be or not to be' speech in German. His lowest Hollywood moment came with *The Klansman*, which he advised Philip Burton not to see: he arrived on the set drunk and remained so throughout the shoot. It is not surprising that he had no memory of the whole enterprise.

Interestingly, his colleagues told me that with any play or film Burton was always at his most brilliant in rehearsal. He was always capable of showing how well he could do what was required: by the time of the show itself he was bored. And here, I think, we have a clue, for perhaps it was not that he had contempt for acting (although he was quickly bored by something that he could do so naturally), but rather that he regarded acting as only one aspect of his personality. Perhaps the essential Richard Burton was the pub performer. Conversation would be scintillating and wide-ranging; the anecdotes would come thick and fast, especially if brother Ivor was in attendance. It was in the pub that he could display all the authority, expertise, humour and charm that he would have brought into play if he had been a preacher, poet or politician. It would have been even more fulfilling if he could have been a don. The truth is that the man who spent the briefest of stays at Oxford was born to be an academic. There is no more poignant photograph of Burton than that of him in a gown talking to Oxford undergraduates, and his calmer moments in his great performance as a history professor in Edward Albee's *Who's Afraid of Virginia Woolf?* indicates what might have been. In his prime the mature Burton exuded a natural authority; it was there in his voice and manner. He could claim his space effortlessly on the stage and in the studio, but he would rather have been doing it for real. The young lad working in the Port Talbot Co-op haberdashery department had spotted that acting was a way out of the rut. It turned out to be something he could do well and it earned him a fortune even as it confirmed that he was indeed a personality. Nevertheless, the career in acting had effectively diverted him from a wider set of issues which had been connected somehow with his native Wales and which had been responsible for having defined the personality which he now undoubtedly was.

That I never saw Richard Burton on stage remains my biggest theatrical regret. I have listened with great envy to the accounts of those who saw his Hal at Stratford or his double act with John Neville at the Old Vic and in particular to those who saw what most critics thought to be his greatest role, that of Coriolanus, the Roman patrician who found it easier to handle the people when they were soldiers than when they became political. Certainly, his Coriolanus was the achievement of which Philip Burton was most proud. When I read what his fellow actor Keith Baxter has to say of Burton on stage I can only sigh at having missed that 'stillness, simplicity, sensitivity and startling vitality'. Baxter refers to a voice 'beautifully modulated' and a 'controlled' physical presence before simply concluding that 'he was a wonderful actor'. All we can do now is to consider whether evidence remains of the magic that many in his live audiences undoubtedly experienced. Nowadays Burton is mostly encountered on random television screenings of his films and all too frequently embarrassment leads to rapid use of the remote control. But occasionally the unmistakable authority in the voice demands attention and I thrill with pleasure at this renewed acquaintance with a well-known friend.

On a desert island I would need to have Burton's *Look Back in Anger*, not because he was the right choice to play Jimmy Porter but because, aged thirty-four, he was at the height of his powers and suggests all the vitality and energy offered by his generation to a country that was not quite ready to respond to the challenge. I would take too *The Prince of Players*, *Cleopatra* and *Becket* chiefly as a hint of what the actor must have been like on stage, but as far as serious film is concerned I would settle for those later films in which an ageing Burton revealed weakness, hollowness, guilt and cynicism. Very brilliantly and sadly the actor exposed both his talents and his inner self in *The Night of the Iguana*, *The Comedians*, *The Spy Who Came in From the Cold* and *Who's Afraid of Virginia Woolf?* I would definitely take the film version of his New York *Hamlet*, which I found to be a total surprise. It may have been crudely made but it certainly reveals some great acting. Here Burton defies many expectations: he is a small, dapper, delicate prince who at first impresses far more with his balletic movements than with his garbled speeches. Gradually we begin to appreciate his great ease and familiarity with the other characters (Keith Baxter asks us to note Burton's unfailing generosity towards his acting partners) and the sheer brilliance of the soliloquies in which every phrase is not only weighted perfectly but highlighted by an entirely appropriate physical gesture. Finally, I would take *Boom*, a movie hated by the critics but one I treasure. In this Joseph Losey version of a Tennessee Williams play, Richard Burton plays an English romantic poet who is also the Angel of Death. On a remote Mediterranean island and wearing a samurai bath-robe he seems to be nothing less than a Greek emperor. But he is also a poet, and as the waves crash against the rocks below he merely says 'boom'. In just one word he conveys everything that the playwright was attempting to say. It is a moment of supreme timing and poetic genius.

And, of course, we have Richard Burton on tape as a reader of verse. 'Ah that voice' is the unfailing reaction of all those who want to claim him as a cultural icon whilst suppressing the knowledge of his everyday life and loves, of all those who want to cherish their own myth rather than that advanced in the tabloids. It is a great voice, although I prefer it in those films in which he issues royal, priestly or military orders rather than reciting verse. By many, he is cherished most as a reader of Dylan Thomas, although personally I find his rendering of the First Voice in *Under Milk Wood* to be too earnest, formal, reverential and churchy, and in general I do not warm to his reading of the poet's individual poems. In 'Fern Hill' he is capable of brilliantly colouring those words 'golden' and 'lordly' that are meant to convey the privileged nature of the young boy but later merely becomes angry and misses all the elegiac subtlety of Dylan's own reading. In other poems you can almost sense his boredom as he longs for more action and drama. He was always at his best reading narrative verse where he could rely on rhyme and rhythm. My first choice for the desert island would be his reading of Coleridge's 'Ancient Mariner' where he superbly colours every word and isolates every image. In his entreaty, 'O shrieve me, shrieve me, holy man', we are not only frightened but we can hear all the wonder and romance that had once made the young Richard Jenkins realize that his future lay in the way he would embrace the language and literature of England.

Almost two decades after his death I still grieve the loss of Richard Burton. He had been a very beautiful and soulful young man who developed a talent to thrill the most demanding audiences and critics in the English-speaking world. The reasons for his subsequent self-destruction are complex and involve the deepest forms of personal, family and sexual guilt. And yet throughout his life there was always a vitality and quickness about him. In those random television sightings as he barks his orders and relishes a word I long to be in one of those Old Vic audiences enjoying him live. Perhaps an even greater regret is not having had the opportunity to sit in on one of his pub performances as he told his tales and enthused about the latest Welsh poet or outside-half. But was he ultimately just a pub Welshman, someone for whom talk was more important than action? Of course he was better than that, for he had done the business at the Old Vic. But should he have done more? Was he in a sense our lost leader? To ask these questions is to highlight the extent to which he let us down. But as we mourn him we mourn a whole society, a society of which he was unquestionably the most tantalizingly brilliant product.

# $S$tanley Baker

'Lovely old Stanley wasn't exactly cultured' is the sentence that leaps out of the rambling, overblown, slightly patronizing and yet moving and revealing tribute penned by Richard Burton in Los Angeles in 1976 when he learnt of the death of his friend Stanley Baker. The essay is dominated by Burton's attempt to show what they, as virtual 'brothers' from a specific south Wales Valleys' culture, had in common even as it gnaws away at the considerable differences between them. The uncultured Baker recalled by his friend was 'tallish, thickish with a face like a determined fist prepared to take the first blow but not the second': he was someone who 'didn't like people very much' and who was 'suspicious to the point of paranoia with strangers'. It sounds as if the author of these judgements, wearing his Anglo-Welsh intellectual's hat, is silently congratulating himself on his less constricted nature and on his fuller love of life and people.

In 1976 Richard Burton still had eight years to live and yet, in that time, he failed to match two notable achievements of Stanley Baker who had been the younger man by three years and who died aged only forty-eight. Burton, Olivier's heir-apparent and the crown prince of the English stage, was, to his intense disappointment, never to be knighted; he had to make do with the notorious runner's-up prize of a CBE. Shortly before his death, however, Stanley Baker was knighted, a recognition of his contribution to the British film industry generally, a reminder of his extensive money-raising work on behalf of various people and projects, and doubtless a consequence of the advice regarding television appearances he had given over the years to prime minister Harold Wilson. Clearly Baker had taken cinema seriously, both as a job and as a business. Even more he had won a place in film mythology, for his 1964 film *Zulu*, which he had helped to set up and in which he starred as the commanding officer at the besieged Rorke's Drift, had caught the public imagination, not least in Wales. He had given Wales a screen hero it could cherish; there was no need for embarrassment here for this was a movie that almost every Welsh film-goer would want on a desert island. This was territory which Burton was not tempted to discuss in his obituary, an appreciation that in one monumental respect tells us much about the author for it contains no mention of acting whatsoever. Here, indeed, is confirmation that Burton did not think in those terms. Meanwhile, Sir Stanley Baker had been not only a professional actor – and proud of that fact – but one with a genuine hinterland.

In 1944 the young Burton and Baker had toured together in Emlyn Williams's *Druid's Rest*. At that time it would have been easy to highlight what they had in common. Baker, too, was a miner's son, a product first of a loving home and then once more of a perceptive and ambitious schoolteacher. At Ferndale Grammar School, Glynne Morse not only supervised Stanley's development as an actor but actually wrote a play for him and took him to Cardiff for auditions and other professional opportunities. In some respects the Rhondda tyro was to achieve recognition more quickly than Philip Burton's protégé from Port Talbot. He was always proud of the fact that his professional career as an actor had started when he was only thirteen and that at only fifteen he had made his first film, playing a boy patriot in a Yugoslavian war drama produced by Ealing and filmed in Breconshire. In the West End, Burton's big break had come in 1949 when he played in Christopher Fry's *The Lady's Not for Burning*. Similarly, Baker always dated his national career from 1951 when he appeared in Fry's *A Sleep of Prisoners* at the St Thomas's Theatre. Many critics thought that this story of four soldiers, prisoners in a bombed church in enemy territory, was the author's best, and T. C. Worsley thought the playing by Leonard White, Denholm Elliott, Hugh Pryse and Stanley Baker was 'quite admirable'. For Baker, as for Burton, West End fame beckoned, but it was not to be and in this respect nature played a part. Baker was a tougher character than his friend, in part because he had experienced a tougher upbringing. Burton had lost his mother but had been spoilt by a loving sister and her husband. Baker had grown up in real poverty for his father had lost a leg in a pit accident and, thereafter, the family had been forced into many expedients to get by. 'Mine is a hell of a face' was to be one of Stanley's oft-quoted remarks, but in fact the young actor had been a good-looker and early stills suggest glamour. Like Burton's, his arrival in the West End occasioned some sexual excitement; certainly the Argentinian novelist Manuel Puig was never to forget his first encounter with Stanley Baker. In motion, however, Baker's appearance always suggested determination, frustration and anger rather than glamour, and the details of the poor upbringing come as no surprise. Somewhat surprisingly there was early praise too for Baker's speaking voice, although it soon became apparent that fine words were not his forte. Glynne Morse was to stress that there were no books in the Baker household: unlike Burton, Baker was not moved to sustain an acting career by a poetic love of language. 'To the end of his life', says biographer Anthony Storey, 'Stanley's spontaneous speech-patterns remained simple, direct sentences with a subject, verb and an object.' But what was more important, as his future wife Ellen had spotted when they first met, 'when Stanley talks he talks with his whole body'. The Welsh Valleys had conjured up two very different acting styles. In a national sporting pantheon, in which both would have chosen to be honoured, the cool rugby back-row forward with his public school and varsity background stands in marked contrast to the gritty, aggressive, never-say-die centre-forward from the local state school.

Richard Burton was a brilliant West End Coriolanus who wanted to be big in the movies, but who was never to find a film persona. Stanley Baker, meanwhile, glided relatively easily into a British film industry desperately anxious to broaden its social range, and particularly eager to match Hollywood's remarkable knack of being able to project entirely appropriate and natural actors in working-class and low-life parts. His early film career was conveniently summed up by Terence Pettigrew who saw him 'shaping up nicely as a competent Hollywood-style "heavy"'; he was 'a lower order tyrant' whose 'rugged physique and short fuse' meant that 'he stuck out like a festered thumb'. He did service as a chauffeur, policeman, 'desert rat', milkman, bo'sun (with Gregory Peck as Hornblower), servant and reporter before achieving some notoriety as the bullying first lieutenant in *The Cruel Sea*. This film's use of melodramatic tension and plain speaking suggested that a new age of British cinematic realism was not far distant. Audiences were shocked, and Baker's cussedness as Bennett, an officer whose duodenal ulcer seems thoroughly deserved, added greatly to the general effect. Thereafter there were to be meatier parts in the same general vein, although his growing stature meant that he could display his anger, energy and sometimes his villainy in costume film as well as contemporary drama, hence his appearance in *Knights of the Round Table* and *Richard III* as well as *Helen of Troy* and (with Richard

Burton) in *Alexander the Great*. At this point British film culture was beginning to ask more serious questions about realism and about the ways in which the energies of actors like Baker could be used. Hitherto, realism had amounted to little more than melodrama and there had been an element of tokenism about the manner in which intruders from the lower orders like Baker had been deployed. Two films made by Baker in that crucial post-Suez, post-John Osborne period did as much as anything to indicate the new energies that British cinema, theatre and television now had to harness.

*Hell Drivers*, made in 1957, was pure melodrama and in some respects, not least in its basic premise, bordered on the absurd. The storyline of rival truck drivers having to risk life and limb in a mad race on dangerous roads had been set up so that two men doing a job could be set against each other *in extremis*. Obviously the incredible intensity, potential danger and violence as well as the psychological rivalry of this movie mark it out as one made within the conventions of American rather than British cinema. Baker plays Yatley, an ex-con trying to go straight and attempting to protect a younger brother, but to survive he has to outwit a psychopathic rival played by Patrick McGoohan. David Thomson has spoken of 'the unexpectedly raw' nature of this film, and it had taken a director from North America to inject this quality into a J. Arthur Rank film. Cy Endfield was a left-wing film-maker who had been active in the Young Communist League whilst a student at Yale and who had worked in the New Theatre League in New York and with Orson Welles before becoming a Hollywood director. Eventually, the House Un-American Activities Committee (HUAC) caught up with him and he fled to London where at first he was forced to work under a pseudonym. It seems entirely appropriate that it was someone with this kind of background who first realized the extent to which Stanley Baker's intensity of pitch could be used to sustain a whole story. Their meeting on this film was providential for they were later to collaborate on a number of ventures, notably *Zulu* in 1964.

In the 1958 film, *Violent Playground*, the subject was juvenile delinquency and Baker played Sgt Truman, a Liverpool detective specific-ally assigned to tackling this problem. This was one of a series of British films made at this time, in which social problems and location shooting were used to give the domestic product the kind of vitality associated with American film. As was so often the case this story collapsed into melodrama, but early on we can sense the production team and the actors striving to launch a new genre. In general this was a path that British cinema was not to take but we can see here the way being paved for what would become the preoccupations and style of British television. Perhaps inevitably, genre was to be the ultimate basis of television drama, with police series always forming the cutting edge in terms of realism, language and acting styles. What was very apparent was that Baker was an ideal British policeman: a working-class chap whose brains and energy had allowed him to make something of himself without ever being able to relax and take anything for granted, he bristles with mistrust as he asserts his authority whilst all the while remaining on the defensive. This was a police officer worthy of promotion and within the year Baker was playing Detective Inspector Morgan in *Blind Date*. More importantly he was now being directed by Joseph Losey, another American radical who had learnt his politics and skills in the New York City of the 1930s and then been driven out of 1950s Hollywood by the McCarthyite witch-hunt. The related themes of class and sexual tension had already begun to characterize Losey's work and not surprisingly his artistic vision was to flourish in England. He and Baker were made for each other, and Baker's Inspector Morgan represents for me a high water mark of American and British cultural intermingling. It took an American director and a chiselling, thrusting Welsh actor to capture the tension inherent in a situation in which a detective hangs on to his own integrity even as he senses all the sexual and physical pleasures on offer in the fashionable and cosmopolitan world in which the crime has taken place. British cinema had been given a new level of resentment and a new range of class and moral perspectives.

Baker had found a niche and in a later age he would surely have starred in a long-running television police series. Meanwhile he returned in 1960 as Inspector Martineau in *Hell is a City*, cleaning up the streets of Manchester but feeling far more at home in the pub where the barmaid has a heart of gold than with his social-climbing wife in the smart suburb. Artistically, however, he had now passed into the hands of Joseph Losey and there is no doubt that the three further films they made together constitute Baker's most interesting work as an actor. *The Criminal*, made in 1960, revealed the harsh realities of organized crime in Britain and Baker's Johnny Bannion, although ultimately destroyed by the big boys, made a lasting impression on domestic audiences who, for the first time, were being made familiar with the psychology of a genuine hardman. Bannion was no stage villain; he was not a cartoon character but rather a driven, Irish Catholic, friendless criminal who wants only his loot. By now Losey was aware of all kinds of energies and possibilities in the actor at his disposal and the time had come to be more ambitious. Losey had become quite fascinated by the sheer brutality of social distinctions and judgements in Britain and his first statement in that respect was to be *The Servant* written by Harold Pinter and made in 1963. Before that he took Stanley Baker to Venice in 1961 to star with Jeanne Moreau in *Eve*. In a superbly photographed baroque city the glitterati and literati mingle at that point in which distinction meets corruption. Flitting around from bar to bar and into the hands of the high-class tart is Tyvian, a successful Welsh novelist from the Valleys. It emerges, however, that Tyvian is a fraud, having hijacked his dead brother's novel. He is after all (and memorably Moreau leaves us with that thought) 'a bloody Welshman' whose nerve, self-loathing and persistence the story needed as the reality of the grossly artificial essence of the hothouse that is Venice was exposed. Six years later in *Accident*, Losey allowed Baker to have genuine qualifications; he was now an Oxford don, albeit one given to appearing on television. The film, again scripted by Pinter, is essentially an exercise in which two dons tear themselves apart, and to sustain this Losey merely exploited the off-screen tension between his two leading actors, the cerebral, refined, elegant, urbane and very English Dirk Bogarde and the physical, athletic, opportunistic Baker.

In his conversations with Michael Ciment, Joseph Losey made the point that it took outsiders like himself, an American mid-westerner, and Harold Pinter, an East End Jew, to pick up on the nuances of English social tensions. Manifestly it had taken an American director to spot the potential of letting loose a Welsh working-class actor, first as a putative novelist at the Venice Biennale and then as a don at exalted Oxford. The casting was so right and the story-line tensions so appropriate that it seems as if Losey and Pinter had seen into the future and were prescribing the way in which Welsh careers would develop. Subsequently, quite a few 'bloody Welshmen' would plague literary festivals and academic conferences and an even greater number of Welsh dons were to irritate senior common rooms and dinner parties alike as they returned from television studios. It is the job of directors and writers to identify actors as they seek to get under the skin of a culture and probe into its possibilities. How one wishes that, at that point, Losey and Pinter had turned their attention more fully to Wales. As it happens Losey had at one stage been under pressure from Sam Spiegel to cast Richard Burton in the part eventually played by Bogarde. Obviously Losey's instincts were sound, for the Bogarde/Baker animosity worked out perfectly. But the notion of Burton and Baker as rival dons, or indeed as rival anything, is mouth-watering, and it is at this stage that one begins to despair at the failure of the film industry in London and the non-existent film industry in Cardiff to exploit these possibilities. As we have seen in the case of Richard Burton, the whole point about actors is that they represent the potentialities of a culture and they are there to prompt producers, director and writers into exciting new territories. Given that actors make their own range very apparent it is entirely legitimate for cultural historians to play the 'if only game': a Losey/Pinter film in which Neath's Ray Milland came home from playing second fiddle to Cary Grant in Hollywood to play a university vice-chancellor at a college where Baker was an ambitious history don (anticipating Malcolm Bradbury's *The History Man*) and Burton a distinguished poet-in-residence with the Rhondda's Donald Houston and Llanelli's Rachel Roberts playing students caught up in some kind of scandal would have done very nicely thank you.

In reality, Richard Burton had settled for being the Welsh ambassador to the world at large. In general he was not going to make anything happen; it was the job of others to set things up for him. Stanley Baker was very different. Burton was at home in California, Switzerland and any Mediterranean or Mexican resort, but Baker, ironically the most American of British actors was, in spite of the many locations and the home in Spain, artistically and financially rooted in London. Unlike Burton, and far more in the manner of Richard Attenborough, he saw movies as his business and consequently set himself up in production. There had to be pluses and minuses in that respect; he produced four films and money was made and quite a lot of money was lost. In his marvellously perceptive and loosely arranged collection of impressionist snapshots of Baker, Anthony Storey describes vividly the movie mogul Baker in his huge office high above the Thames negotiating with South African bankers as he planned the making of *Zulu Dawn*, the sequel to his earlier success. Baker was 'self-contained, quiet, confident' and made his points 'crisply and succinctly'. Meanwhile the critics were divided. Some had regretted his emergence as an art-house player and were glad to see him occasionally playing good old-fashioned villains again as he did in his production of *Robbery*, the story of the great train heist. Others, such as David Thomson, regretted the way in which the actor lost out to the entrepreneur; his parts were not well chosen and in his own productions, even *Zulu*, 'his thoughts seemed fixed on the papers in his office'.

At least, and for this we must be grateful, Stanley Baker had time to give some consideration to Wales. What was most pleasing about his relationship with Wales was that it was entirely lacking in affectation. He was a poor boy from the Rhondda who had succeeded in London but who retained total respect and an enormous affection for what he had been given by his family and friends. He would roar down to Wales in his Jaguar, waving to all his mates in the Rhondda streets. One of my most treasured screen memories of him is that moment when he stood above the deserted pit in Jack Howells's television film *Return to the Rhondda* and, pointing down, explains 'my father lost his leg down there'. He was, as Burton emphasized, 'inwrought with his valley', and there was also the impression that, given any kind of opportunity, in other words given good scripts, he would have wanted to have done more with Wales cinematically. Nevertheless, he did enough to retain the respect and admiration of that south Wales community of which he was so unmistakably a product. Over the years he did a number of television plays in Wales but, in particular, his Welsh laurels were earned first for *Zulu*, a movie (as Lady Ellen Baker pointed out) he produced when he was still in his early thirties, and then for the BBC's 1976 production of *How Green Was My Valley*. What we see in this respect is Baker confirming his Welsh identity and cementing his links with his natural Welsh constituency by using material at hand, material that was the product of a wider set of circumstances. *Zulu* was based on a John Prebble story and was scripted by Prebble and the co-producer/director Cy Endfield. It was, as Dave Berry argues, a fairly conventional adventure film with the most interesting strand, the class tension between Baker's Lieutenant Chard and Michael Caine's Lieutenant Bromhead, owing much to the American influences surrounding Baker at that time. It was, however, a stunning film to look at and the sight of the red uniforms on the veld together with all the verbal and musical references to Wales were enough to catch the imagination of a Welsh film-going audience who had been denied the historical mythology that should have been truly theirs. This was, as Dai Smith argued, the great Welsh western. Over the years thousands of Welshmen have sought adventure by putting on red or khaki uniforms, but *Zulu* remains the only movie that ever spoke directly to that segment of the nation's imagination. In turning to *How Green Was My Valley* the BBC were utilizing a novel written in 1939 by Richard Llewellyn, a London Welshman with little direct experience of Wales, and which had already been filmed in Hollywood in 1941 as well as by the BBC in 1959. This 1976 version had very little of Hollywood's slickness and was artistically torpedoed by having different actors play the young Huw in successive episodes, but nevertheless it struck many chords in south Wales which was just at that stage of losing its coal-mining industry. Emrys Jones, the Labour Party's agent in Wales, made a point of stressing to me 'how much more of this kind of thing we need'. As he enthused about the programme he made it clear that it was Stanley Baker as the father who was carrying the whole venture. The actor was dying of cancer and looked years older than his actual age of forty-eight. It was painful to watch this performance given all our vivid memories of that dark, saturnine, strutting dynamo of just a decade or so earlier. But what was never in question was that this Gwilym Morgan was the genuine article, a true and classic Welsh patriarch, prematurely aged by a life underground. We should not really have been surprised by Lady Ellen's explanation to Anthony Storey that in this series the actor was consciously 'playing his father'. The Rhondda miner, who had never seen his son on the stage and who died before the great success story unfolded, was now commemorated in the most personal and enduring form. Furthermore this role, essentially Baker's last, was truly an epitaph for his valley and all the other valleys too.

In these last years there were to be many press references to Baker's efforts to set up a film version of *Rape of the Fair Country*, Alexander

Cordell's 1959 novel set in the early nineteenth-century iron towns at the heads of the Valleys. Unfortunately, the rights to this work had been acquired by an American company and, regrettably, Baker's illness and subsequent death prevented a successful outcome to these negotiations. Here again it is revealing that the text would have been a popular novel by an outsider, albeit one whose sheer sense of lusty vitality had done more to arouse an interest in the story of Welsh industrialization than anything written by any Welsh historian or novelist. Again Baker's instincts had enabled him to see how his own business interests and understanding of Welsh popular idiom could be usefully conjoined. As is so often the case with the Welsh screen giants of that era, one wishes that somehow Welsh money and Welsh literary and academic expertise could have been at hand. The richness of our history has been well and truly ignored and, yet, as Richard Llewellyn, Alexander Cordell and the agent of the Welsh Labour Party knew, the public were crying out for their history to be explained and at that particular moment in time, as the industrial era began to expire, they had every reason to call for their culture to respond.

In time, as movies became fashionable and cineastes began to treasure as classical what had largely been taken for granted, Stanley Baker's career was reappraised. Even before his death David Thomson emphasized that 'he is one of Britain's most important screen actors', and a later generation of critics had no difficulty in agreeing with that judgement. In their programme notes for a season of Baker's films at Cardiff's Chapter cinema David Prothero and Tony Whitehead referred to his 'incandescent talent' and justifiably pointed out that his 'body of work is by far the most impressive of any Welsh actor'. He had grown up in Wales but loved Hollywood and he, more than any other British actor, injected Hollywood-like energies into what had been a one-paced British cinema. He was a chiseller from the wrong side of the tracks, but he was also a quintessential Welsh coal miner forcing various English actors to come to terms with an obduracy that they had previously only associated with industrial relations. We had sent him as an intruder into a different culture and he did not let us down. We let him down, though, because we had not provided the stories and the histories that he could have fleshed out. We must watch his movies now because they are our history.

# $R$achel Roberts

That show business could be hell was never a secret. Those of us who have been enthralled by the movies and theatre, aware of all the intellectual and emotional thrills on offer (and perhaps just a little bit in love with a number of stars), will have been frequently reminded that it was not all glamour and glitz. We had no excuse for not knowing that actors were highly vulnerable, that they had opted for careers in which they would be fully exposed, frequently disappointed and ultimately very much on their own with nowhere to hide. With most good actors we did not see or consciously analyse the skills that formed the basis of their performances but, in the back of our minds, we must have been aware of how actors needed supreme discipline and control if they were to combine their profession with successful lives generally.

There were some actors whose work and careers constantly reminded us of the pressures they were under. As far as men were concerned a new generation of actors like Brando and Dean were portraying vulnerability and sexual ambivalence. More than anything, though, it was Montgomery Clift's career which led one to wonder for the first time whether acting actually attracted people who were consciously or unconsciously seeking help or at least confirmation of their identity. At the same time we were given every reason to believe that things were even more difficult for women. For years her fans took Judy Garland's films and concerts as a running exposure not only of her own problems but as general comment on the epic struggle necessarily awaiting talented women who opted for careers in the public eye. Films such as *A Star is Born* (1954) and *I Could Go on Singing* (1963) were cautionary yet compellingly gruesome tales that could be imagined as deterring some young girls from a career in show business. In 1963 Judy Garland was forty-one and had six years left to live but Marilyn Monroe had already gone: she had died in 1962 aged only thirty-six. As we began to consider the details of her life and death the full horror began to dawn of how it was possible for someone to be essentially alone and unprotected even in the midst of life at its apparently most glamorous.

It was tempting to see this phenomenon as being very American. Indeed, long before Kenneth Anger filled in the details in his *Hollywood*

*Babylon* books, we had realized that the hills behind Sunset Boulevard were far from innocent and seldom joyful. And, in time, even British complacency was to be shaken, as it became apparent that the power of show biz to destroy was not a purely Californian phenomenon. I remember seeing the Glaswegian actress Mary Ure on stage at Stratford where she was a strikingly blonde and innocent Desdemona murdered by Paul Robeson's authentically black Othello, and then a little later she moved me greatly as the soft, vulnerable, hard-done-by wife scathingly denounced by Richard Burton's Jimmy Porter in the film of John Osborne's *Look Back in Anger*. In 1975 Mary Ure died at the age of forty-two from a mix of alcohol and barbiturates. Just two years earlier I had seen Rachel Roberts in Friedrich Dürrenmatt's play *The Visit* and had taken particular pleasure in being able to enjoy the triumph of a girl from my part of Wales in a Broadway production. Within seven years she had taken her own life in those notorious Hollywood hills. Ten years later her friend Jill Bennett whom I had seen on stage in the West End in *Time Present*, a play by her then husband John Osborne, committed suicide, thereby allowing her one-time partner to embark on the most famous character assassination in theatre history. Obviously British theatre was not all sweetness and light, and not all British actresses were untroubled cultural adornments.

Wales is a small country, its artistic community smaller still, and so Rachel Roberts's death was keenly felt. As in any tightly knit family a suicide had collective consequences; it prompted guilt and much 'if only' speculation. In any overwhelmingly peasant society women tended to enter public life in a limited number of occupations and, in those occupations, whether it be teaching, music or theatre, their contributions had been characterized by a no-nonsense and confident professionalism. Above all it was teaching which set the tone for women in Welsh public life and for several generations the job determined norms of dress and speech and an ethos of plain common sense. A related role was that of the minister's wife. Interestingly, Rachel Roberts's mother had been, in the time-honoured phrase, 'a wonderful help' to her husband in Swansea and, apparently, a better speaker than her Baptist minister husband. Over the years quite a few teachers and potential teachers realized that it took only a little more nerve to transfer their communication skills to the stage and screen. Much depended on opportunity, and one teacher who had already taken hers was the miner's daughter Rachel Thomas who went from a Cardiff classroom straight into the film *The Proud Valley* and thereafter maintained an almost exclusive monopoly on the role of the Welsh mam. Rachel Thomas thus embarked on a public career in which she made it official that Welsh women were above all mothers, that they ruled in the kitchen and were always available for the dispensing of affection, balanced judgement and wry asides. Essentially, Rachel Thomas had been a product of that teacher-led wave of popular drama which had swept through the Wales of the 1930s. That somewhat surprising cultural manifestation had been meant as an antidote to unemployment and its attendant privation; it had certainly not been devised as a recipe for personal anguish. In the popular enthusiasm for theatre the subsequent despair of Rachel Roberts could not have been envisaged.

Knowing some of the horribly gruesome details of Rachel Roberts's awful lonely death in distant Los Angeles, I was reluctant to read Alexander Walker's 'documentary biography' of her which incorporates the actress's own journals and diary. It was a volume I often picked up and then just as regularly put down. Eventually I found it to be as sad and sobering as expected but, as a biography, *No Bells on Sunday* is a magnificent achievement. Walker's insights and his use of many interviews combined with the actress's own unstinting honesty to provide as full a portrait of an actor's life and ultimate failure as we have ever been given. The story is one of an actress losing control, of hopeless addiction to sex and alcohol, of a growing dependence on stimulants and prescription drugs, of a collapsing professional confidence and finally, of course, of loneliness. 'You'll be left alone', her mother had warned in the way that Welsh mothers would. Walker and Rachel herself guide us through all these stages with full details of public humiliation and private anguish. As is always the case with accounts of boorish drunken behaviour there is a danger of all sympathy being lost. Yet though we are shown many moments of messy and squalid hopelessness there are, too, ample opportunities for admiring the ways in which she sustained a career which has to be celebrated in the pantheon of Welsh acting.

Rachel, or Ray as she was known to her friends, wrote superbly, and the prose in her journals, including some snippets of fiction, suggest that she might easily have developed into a novelist. Her honesty and remarkable degree of self-knowledge prove that she had the qualities necessary to flesh out sophisticated fiction and her feel for the telling phrase is very apparent. One of her characters sensed that 'the medieval face of Catholic Italy had a density; you walked in an atmosphere; life itself was thick', whilst a fictionalized version of Richard Burton 'had a face that Michelangelo would want to sculpt'. Writer manqué she might have been, but what we can say of Rachel Roberts is that she was every inch a professional actor. To follow the details of her working life is to be amazed by the resilience and toughness of an actor who never stinted in the pursuit of pleasure or escape but then always ensured that she was on time for the rehearsal or the actual show. Her nights on the tiles were not allowed to affect her work and this was appreciated by her colleagues. She was frequently extremely apprehensive before a play opened, but once in her part she would invariably flourish. She knew that she was 'a working actress' and was fastidious about not breaking the rules in that respect. Only once did she fail, withdrawing from an Athol Fugard play as she began what was later interpreted as her final descent into despair.

What is immensely moving in her analysis of her career is the rather old-fashioned and unaffected reverence for the skill which had made her professional career possible. She speaks of 'her beloved talent' and of how in her prime she had possessed faith and confidence in it. Frequently, and with obvious echoes of Dylan Thomas, she would refer to 'her craft'. She was also fully conscious of whence that craft had come. Her father had been a minister capable of *hwyl*, and her mother was an excellent speaker, but they were less important than her paternal grandfather, a preacher named Goronwy Owen Rhys Roberts, from whom she inherited her pug nose, her good voice and much else beside. Near the end she spoke of having inherited from Grandpa her 'birthright', 'my voice and Welsh emotionalism, my acting'.

Rachel Roberts's tragedy was that, for her, acting was not enough, was not sufficient reward in itself. There had to be something more and for a glorious decade in mid-career that something extra was provided by Rex Harrison. The theme of both Alexander Walker's biography and David Howard's 1998 television portrait is that the actress realized that her whole career had rested on a Rex-or-work dilemma; she was never sure which had formed the core of her existence. After her marriage to Rex came to an end her life was never as meaningful and she found it difficult to re-engage fully with her craft. In her final disorder she was more than ever preoccupied with memories of Rex and with forlorn hopes of a reunion. Clearly Rex had in some respects swept her off her feet, not least with his lifestyle with which she was as totally fascinated as only a Baptist from Swansea could be. Rex, a stockbroker's son from Liverpool, had played cricket at school and had developed in provincial repertory into the quintessence of English charm. Rachel loved his pure English class, but even more she appreciated all the things to which his post-*My Fair Lady* wealth and celebrity had given him access. It was to be a marriage sustained by champagne, first-class hotels, first-class service, first-class travel and an idyllic Mediterranean retreat above Portofino. When the marriage ended all these things were badly missed; after all Rachel had felt that she was entitled to them.

This notion of her having earned the good life with Rex was a crucial part of her self-analysis. She was constantly noting the success of those fellow-actors with whom she identified, the acclaimed Joan Plowright and Maggie Smith, and concluding that she had been very different. For her, acting had never been an end in itself but rather the way in which she, a second-favourite child, someone perpetually disappointed with her own looks (especially her nose) and unmistakably a product of industrial south Wales, could make some impact. She was from the very beginning a rebel, a daredevil, the classic daughter of the manse who was out to shock. Her clothes, her drinking, her sex life and the choice of career announced her as a premature 'beatnik'. Yet, she took her job utterly seriously and it would be her success at that job which would allow her status as a personality. Throughout her journals she linked herself with Peter O'Toole and Richard Burton, for all three of them were actors who 'wanted not only to impress, but to dominate'. Underneath there were fears and uncertainties but, meanwhile, there was the enormous satisfaction of being the centre of attention, of being cherished by others as a great personality. As with Richard Burton a lesson had to be painfully learnt, for it is difficult to sustain one's status as a show-biz or cultural personality if one breaks with the basic conventions and constraints which govern a professional actor's life. With acting it is probably going too far to say that one is only as good as one's last performance, but nevertheless the status of a star should only be judged by artistic contributions made within the developing logic and culture of contemporary theatre and cinema.

The tragedy was that Rachel Roberts, having made a distinctive mark as an actor, went on to provide yet another example of a Welsh star being diverted from artistic fulfilment. From the University College of Wales at Aberystwyth she had gone to RADA where she was a prizewinner. After seasons at Swansea and Stratford she caught the eye as Emilia in Burton's *Othello* at the Old Vic. National fame came in 1960 when she played opposite Albert Finney in Karel Reisz's film *Saturday Night and Sunday Morning*. Her contribution to this landmark 'kitchen-sink' film was considerable. British cinema was experimenting with realism and was very aware of its obligation to reflect the new working-class and provincial energies expressed in the novels, plays and rock music of the 1950s. It needed new stories, new locations and above all new actors to catch the mood of this new generation. Albert Finney, an actor from Salford who had impressed at Stratford, was to take his chance well. His truculent, cocksure factory worker was perfectly pitched to win over all those young people and critics who had previously thought that only American actors could play rebels convincingly. Meanwhile, Rachel had been handed the potentially difficult role of the married woman with whom the hero is having an affair; in the film she becomes pregnant, has an abortion and is abandoned by her lover who goes off with a more attractive, younger girlfriend. Traditionally English actresses had failed to convince in proletarian settings, and it is difficult to imagine anyone other than Rachel Roberts being able to make a convincing whole out of all the elements in the part of Brenda. Several local authorities were shocked by the most explicit bedroom scenes yet seen in a British film, and yet Brenda had combined her sexual allure and pleasure with later scenes of careworn frumpiness. We knew from the hollowness in the eyes that this woman was a loser, but we were unable to forget the fun she had during that night in the pub when her feelings for her lover, her pride in him, had been very obvious. There is a haunting pathos here, and it is a performance that I cannot get out of my mind.

Not content with this role of Brenda, she was later to play the widow Mrs Hammond in Lindsay Anderson's 1963 film *This Sporting Life*. This was without question one of the best performances in that whole cycle of British 'kitchen-sink' films and it received almost universal acclaim. Critics soon spotted that this was not a run-of-the-mill sociological melodrama. Only superficially was this a film about sport and all the shots of the rugby field, the terraces and the changing rooms were merely a backcloth to a detailed and intense study of two people locked into a tragic moment of truth. Anderson rehearsed the film as if it were a play and chose his stars with great care. Richard Harris played Machin, the former miner who finds some kind of fulfilment and also an outlet for his aggression in professional rugby, whilst Rachel Roberts plays his austere and even grim landlady with whom he becomes preoccupied. The relationship between Machin and Mrs Hammond is utterly tragic and was almost as painful to endure for the audiences as it must have been for the characters themselves. There is nothing like it in British cinema and many critics identified the film as one intended by its director to take its place in the European *nouvelle vague*. Mrs Hammond has one major speech at the graveside but otherwise the relationship is based on haunted agonizing stares. If there was an English tradition to which this kind of emotional torture and depth of silent passion belonged it had been provided by D. H. Lawrence. Penelope Gilliatt of the *Observer* was one of the critics who spotted this: she reported that she had 'never seen an English picture that gave such expression to the violence and the capacity for pain that is in the English character'. Alexander Walker was to refer to 'the Lawrence-like passions of puritan denial eating worm-like throughout it'. On the set everyone was taken aback with the actress's clenched intensity. Richard Harris said in admiration: 'She is Welsh, a Celt, sensitive. She knows it all. She's so good you don't have to act with her.' *Newsweek* talked of how she 'manages to project oceans of suppressed passion'.

At the time I saw Rachel Roberts on Broadway, the New York critic Clive Barnes was praising a performance of *The Widowing of Mrs Holroyd* at Newhaven's Long Wharf Theatre and making the point that in D. H. Lawrence, who had died in 1930, the 1970s might have found its most significant dramatist. I went to Connecticut to see the play and was indeed overwhelmed by the power of this genuinely proletarian and authentically kitchen-sink drama. Joyce Ebert was excellent, but I could not help thinking that Rachel Roberts would have been superb as Mrs

Holroyd, whose dead husband's body was brought back from the pit and laid out on the kitchen table. The revival of Lawrence's plays had begun at London's Royal Court Theatre in the late 1960s. The Royal Court, of course, had been at the cutting edge of British theatre since George Devine's English Stage Company had taken over in 1956. In 1959 Alan Dobie, the actor Rachel had married in 1955, appeared at the Royal Court in *Sergeant Musgrave's Dance* directed by Lindsay Anderson. From that time on she was to have a spiritual home in London with Lindsay Anderson who became, as *No Bells on Sunday*, fully documents, her lifelong friend and guru. In the most savage of all ironies Rachel, already separated from Dobie, was to star at the Royal Court in a 1960 production of Chekhov's *Platonov* with Rex Harrison in the title role. In her very first role in the intimate Sloane Square Theatre which should have become her working base and where, like Joan Plowright, she could have begun an ascent to the peak of her profession, she fell under the power of a man who not only took her away but who had little or no respect for the kind of acting that necessarily went on in the avant-garde plays staged by Devine, Anderson, Tony Richardson, John Osborne and the rest of the Royal Court team.

Her marriage to Rex Harrison was well and truly over when Rachel returned to the Royal Court in 1972 to star with Albert Finney in E. A. Whitehead's new play *Alpha Beta*, directed by Anthony Page, yet another professional associate who became a friend and adviser to the actress. In this play, Rachel was back at the forefront of new theatre and as far removed as possible from the glamour that Rex Harrison had thought natural and desirable. The play traces the destruction of a marriage over a twelve-year period. In her role as Mrs Elliot, for which she won the *Evening Standard* Best Actress Award, Rachel had to fight it out round for round with her husband, all the while expressing bitterness, contempt, hatred, jealousy and hopelessness. The performance was filmed, but perhaps it is the production stills which most fully convey the intensity the author required and the sheer gloom of Rachel's characterization. In some of John Haynes's photographs she seems to be expressing a Neanderthal ferocity, and one angry glance as she washes the dishes serves as the eternal last word on kitchen-sink.

A colleague of Rachel's once spoke of 'her one visible weakness'

this *Observer* review that she had worked for him at Greenwich. What he does mention, and obviously with distaste, is her background. This half-Welsh writer (Osborne was once referred to as 'a Welsh Fulham upstart') was obviously irritated by Rachel's 'Welsh-warbling' and by the way the book did not allow the reader to forget that she was 'born in Wales'.

Plainly intending to be dismissive Osborne identified Rachel as 'a character actress'. Ultimately that is precisely what she had become, a thoroughly professional actress who was capable of injecting more despair, pain and anger into her parts than any other British actress, and clearly more than many British men could take. She was able to convey those 'oceans of passion', in part because of her intelligence (Sybil Christopher said that as an actress she was 'tenaciously academic') and in part because as a manic-depressive she had much on which to draw. As the plain girl from Wales fought fiercely to make her mark in a world in which she knew in her heart that she would always be an outsider, she honed a considerable talent but at the same time acquired considerable needs. She had become wholly dependent on men, booze and drugs. And, of course, people who need these most tend, as her Swansea mother had warned, to end up on their own, in this case horribly on their own.

# *H*ugh Griffith

After reliving the tempestuous *Sturm und Drang* elements in the lives of Burton and Roberts and recalling the restless anger of Baker's films, it is something of a relief to turn to the sense of fulfilment in the career of Hugh Griffith. The Anglesey-born actor lived a very full sixty-eight years and, in that time, gave considerable pleasure to both theatre and film audiences. The consistently appreciative reviews of his work alongside those profiles in which he highlighted his interest in golf, farming, property development and breeding corgis reinforce the conclusion that we are dealing here with perhaps the most worthwhile and successful Welsh acting career. And, of course, it was satisfactorily and justifiably rewarded with that 1959 Oscar.

That breeding of corgis is important because it reminds us of the element of balance and perspective in Griffith's career. Recalling T. C. Worsley's perceptive comment in 1951 that Richard Burton had made his mark 'too early for his own good', it is almost refreshing to note that after Llangefni Grammar School Hugh Griffith worked in a bank for eight years and was already twenty-six when he won his Leverhulme scholarship to RADA. Having won the Bancroft Gold Medal at RADA he made his West End debut in 1939, but then spent six years in the Royal Welch Fusiliers, including time in India, before returning to the stage in 1946 when he was thirty-four. What a wonderful change from all that usual emphasis on Celtic youthfulness and adolescent promise and how utterly refreshing to contemplate the professional work of a Welsh actor who had lived not only a full but a real life.

By the time of his death in 1980 Griffith was treasured as a larger-than-life personality, a truly theatrical character whose huge eyes, pre-Cambrian nose and totally unaffected Welsh cattle-mart rhetoric had made him one of the country's most recognizable actors and one capable of stealing any film: in truth he was always 'the best supporting actor'. In *Ben Hur* his Oscar-winning performance was truly wonderful; with every viewing I am struck by the way that the star players, the horses, the chariots and the settings are all less vivid than the flashing eyes and teeth of Griffith's Sheikh Ilderim. He has all the best lines and his pen-etratingly shrill voice enables him to give them a real edge. 'One God I can understand', he tells the Romans whom he cleverly patronizes and outmanoeuvres, 'but one wife! That is uncivilized.' In the wonderful baths scene in which he makes his bet with the naked Romans he greets them (and this is one of Hollywood's most memorably delivered lines) as 'You Protectors of our far-flung marshes, masters of the earth'. In George MacDonald Fraser's view 'there never was an Arab sheikh to touch Hugh Griffith'. In *Khartoum* Olivier as the Mahdi rolled his eyes and his tongue, but he has to take second place in the Orientalist pantheon of acting. Meanwhile Hugh carried on with a busy film career, and he was to be at his most memorable as Squire Western in *Tom Jones* and as the mayor in the BBC's 1972 version of *Clochemerle*.

It is gratifying that the actor enjoyed such a lengthy and busy film career, but the notion of Griffith as a scene-stealing 'larger-than-life' personality tends to eclipse the fact that he had earlier developed a remarkably successful and varied career in the theatre. His later wealth and fame were based on skills and techniques, especially those related to timing and voice projection, which he had learnt in an acclaimed theatrical career, at first as an amateur on Anglesey and then professionally. He was not, of course, the only product of the Llangefni Little Theatre to achieve fame, for his sister Elen Roger Jones was to have a distinguished acting career in Wales. Before the war there had been a Celtic dimension to Griffith's work. In the West End he appeared in Synge's *The Playboy of the Western World* and then starred as the Revd Dan Price in the theatrical version of Jack Jones's *Rhondda Roundabout* which had a short run on Shaftesbury Avenue. After the war he went straight to the reopened theatre at Stratford where he played six roles including Touchstone in *As You Like It*, Holofernes in *Love's Labour's Lost* and Trinculo in *The Tempest*, as well as Mephistopheles in *Doctor Faustus*. In 1946 he was in Webster's *The White Devil* in London: his Monticelso was, said Kenneth Tynan, 'superbly degenerate'. In 1949 he was in the title role of *King Lear* in Swansea's Grand Theatre and, famously, he starred in *Y Brenin Llŷr*, Dafydd Gruffydd's production of his father W. J. Gruffydd's translation for the BBC. Later he would identify this Everest of Shakespearean roles as his favourite. The audience at the Grand had been fortunate to see this 37-year-old Lear but we must all regret that there was to be no reprise in later decades.

In 1951 he was back at Stratford for their Festival of Britain season and this time he landed juicy roles in which he could invest something of himself. T. C. Worsley thought that he 'richly points the prophetic strain' in John of Gaunt's great speech, although elsewhere some of his sentences faded into inaudibility; in *The Tempest* he was a 'veritable mooncalf' of a Caliban. His third part that summer was in one of the most memorable productions of *Henry IV Part I* with Anthony Quayle as the king, Michael Redgrave as Hotspur and Richard Burton as Hal. Griffith, of course, was Glendower, surely a part he was born to play: what other Welsh actor was ever to come near to suggesting that the character was 'extraordinary not in the role of common men' and indeed that at his birth 'the goats ran from the mountains'? Using one word to speak volumes Worsley described his performance as 'portentous'. Inevitably, this production had a particularly Welsh flavour with Burton and Griffith encouraging each other in their Welshness. In his biography of Burton Melvyn Bragg does full justice to Griffith as he explains how the younger actor always loved to hear anecdotes about Hugh, who had played practical jokes on him at Stratford. Pulling out all the stops, Bragg evokes a Griffith with 'a body big as a mattress' and 'a face like an Easter Island statue whose mother had mated with a gargoyle'. Some critics pointed out that, as Hal, Burton had overdone the Welsh accent. Naturally Griffith made the most of his Welsh-language speeches, although Sybil Burton who was playing his daughter needed special coaching from husband Richard before mastering her responses. For the seven-month season the Burtons stayed with Hugh Griffith and his wife Adelgunde at Oxhill where they held riotous parties. There were many occasional visitors including Humphrey Bogart whom Burton's brother Graham remembers expressing the desire to play Shakespearean roles. Visitors could not help but notice that there was a Welsh dragon on display in every room and that the corgis who shepherded visitors around the house only obeyed instructions when called by name – Branwen, Olwen or, most mischievously, Matholwch. Adelgunde was a superb cook and the actor Robert Hardy described the house, ten miles outside Stratford, as 'a Welsh country club', but nevertheless 'a mad house' too.

Hugh Griffith certainly gave full value for money at Stratford, but it was in the plays of Jean Anouilh that he received most critical acclaim.

The French writer was 'all the rage' in the post-war period with Harold Hobson describing him as 'the finest theatrical writer of his time'. Griffith was to make a substantial contribution to the process whereby the playwright's reputation was secured. In 1950 Anouilh's *Eurydice* was presented at the Lyric Hammersmith as *Point of Departure* and the production was greeted with an ecstatic critical response: the retelling of the Orpheus story was powerful and magical. There was praise for Dirk Bogarde and Mai Zetterling as Orpheus and Eurydice and also for Hugh Griffith as the father. Worsley thought his playing of 'a seedy, creased old man', for whom life is still worth living and for whom 'the everyday pleasures of the sensual life' allow 'the miracle of re-growth', a 'virtuoso display'. However, his great success is best evoked by Harold Hobson who relished the way in which 'the downhearted wandering harpist rolls his tongue over the consolations of life': this 'savouring of pleasure' was 'the apotheosis of aperitifs and cheap cigars'. Later in the year the play, renamed as *Legend of Lovers*, opened in New York with Richard Burton and Dorothy McGuire in the leading roles. The production flopped and was taken off after only two weeks, but there had been time for Burton to impress in his first American lead and for Hugh Griffith, who once more played the father, to bequeath Broadway one of its most treasured anecdotes. Hating this new interpretation of the play Griffith had stormed out and announced that he was going home. But Pier 90 was deserted; the *Queen Mary* had sailed. Burton spotted him sheepishly returning to the hotel and said: 'Thought you were going home.' 'Dammit', came the reply, 'I'm not Jesus. I can't walk the bloody Atlantic!' American consolation would come six years later when he starred on Broadway in Ketti Fring's adaptation of Thomas Wolfe's novel *Look Homeward Angel*. The young Thomas was played by Anthony Perkins with Griffith as his father. The *International Theatre Annual* critic George Alan Smith, having inevitably picked out 'England's Hugh Griffiths', highlighted the scene in which the father gleefully tears down the boarding-house porch: 'doubtless' this will 'linger through a lifetime of theatrical memory'. The actor had swung 'into the towering drunken rage with a demonic energy and raving-eyed fire that is hard to forget'. A story that Richard Burton always cherished has Griffith being nominated for a Tony Award only to be asked if he was a method actor. 'No, no', he explained, 'but I am a Methodist.'

Meanwhile in London he had again made his mark in an Anouilh play. In 1956 his playing of the ageing General Saint-Pé in *The Waltz of the Toreadors* was adjudged by the *International Theatre Annual* to be one of the best performances of the year, one conceived, according to J. W. Lambert, with 'loving skill and gentle relish'. What this critic appreciated was the way the bearded, blinking Griffith revealed that the general's pain was not just that of 'an elderly rake or a retired soldier sniffing his youth' but rather that of a man unable to escape 'the cruelty of moral cowardice'. It was in the late 1950s that his film career began to take off but he remained very much a man of the theatre, and an actor still very much at the cutting edge of the national theatrical scene. In 1962 he played at the Aldwych in the Royal Shakespeare Company's production of Brecht's *Caucasian Chalk Circle*. Tynan found that his 'scrambled delivery' somewhat marred the play's 'almost Shakespearean-roistering ambiguities' but, nevertheless, Hugh Griffith's performance as Azdak was 'otherwise irresistible'.

In 1964 he was back at Stratford playing several major roles including one that undoubtedly represented the highlight of his theatrical career. In Peter Hall's production of the two *Henry IV*s he played Falstaff to Ian Holm's Hal. Ronald Bryden disliked the Brechtian aspects of the production but adjudged this Falstaff as 'the best I've ever seen'. The critic conceded that the actor's creation was essentially 'a stage conception, as formal and artificial as Punch or Dame Twanky, impossible to imagine outside a theatre', yet it kept 'bursting into vitality, slyness and real danger'. The element of danger was crucial, of course, for whilst this production sacrificed none of the play's comedy this Falstaff was no 'dissolute Santa', as was so often the case; he was indeed 'a tempter, a menace to throne and state'. Hal had to be on his guard and in his rejection of the old man he had to be firm. Hugh Griffith's performance is best evoked and most fully acclaimed by T. F. Wharton in his 1983 volume in the Text and Performance series. He argues that it was basically 'a simple interpretation', yet one that ideally suited the production for in turn it was 'gleeful, tender, crafty, baleful'. All in all Wharton thought it an unforgettable experience; there was 'the large physical presence, the roaring, braying, gargling voice with its great sensual range' and above all 'the glittering eyes and sharp features' giving 'the head a curious eagle-like appearance, atop the enormous body'.

Wharton recalled 'a noisy performance, far from word perfect' but one that 'swept the play along with an unstoppable gusto'. But for all the boisterousness it was the elegiac quality which stood out, not least in the Tavern scene when Falstaff gazes for some time into the fire and then instructs Doll Tearsheet (Susan Engel), whose head lies on his shoulder: 'do not speak like a death's head; do not bid me remember mine end.'

Memorable he may have been at Stratford, but for most people in the 1960s and 1970s Hugh Griffith had become one of the most familiar character actors on the big screen. Almost predictably he would crop up in gothic films, stories set in the Middle East or routine domestic comedies to provide cameo performances in which his eyes and voice would be used to full effect. His professor was the best thing in the 1957 film of *Lucky Jim*, the kind of role which should have been repeated. Whenever I walk through Swansea University's Singleton Abbey I half expect Griffith's Professor Welch to emerge from a corridor and order me back to the library. Undoubtedly his Squire Western in the much acclaimed *Tom Jones*, starring Albert Finney, and then his mayor in the BBC's *Clochemerle* were his most satisfactory and satisfying roles. In *Clochemerle* he provided television viewers with one of the great comic moments of the era. In the small Beaujolais town all the residents and the brass band lingered restlessly in the square as they waited for the mayor's bladder to function to mark the official opening of the town's new *pissoir*; only after an agonizing wait did the flow come. In these adaptations of novels by Henry Fielding and Gabriel Chevalier Hugh Griffith was perfectly cast, for this native of Anglesey was a rural rather than an urban man. He was a peasant, although a grand one, rather than a besuited office worker. Squire Western was spot-on, for Hugh Griffith was essentially a kulak, a peasant farmer who had done well by outsmarting his rivals at the local auctions, cattle marts and horse fairs. Those eyes were meant to clinch deals, that nose to smell bargains and that voice to berate opponents. In my childhood I was a devotee of the Twm Shon Catti cartoon strips and subsequently I always envisaged Hugh Griffith as a farmer in those stories.

*Clochemerle* remains an important clue, for Hugh Griffith was undoubtedly the most truly international of all the great Welsh actors. If he was familiar with the Roman Empire's 'far-flung marshes' he could also boast about his days in Tahiti where he went in 1962 to act in

*Mutiny on the Bounty* alongside Marlon Brando, Trevor Howard, Richard Harris and assorted rats, scorpions and land crabs. It was perhaps inevitable that this most continental of Welshmen should establish a niche in classic European cinema. He started to appear in Italian films as early as 1965 but it was his participation in the Italian-French co-production of *The Canterbury Tales* in 1972 that will be recalled as his most significant excursion into the exotic, not to say the erotic. In 1971 the great Marxist director Pier Paolo Pasolini embarked on a trilogy in which he intended to glorify the peasants of the Middle Ages and to show that sex could be natural and joyful when released from what Robin Buss termed 'the repressive mechanisms of bourgeois political and family life'. The first instalment, in which the director himself played Giotto, was a bawdy but nevertheless effective and humorous rendering of Boccaccio's tales. In contrast *The Canterbury Tales*, in which Pasolini played Chaucer, was roundly condemned for having forfeited all the poet's subtlety in the interest of titillation. One critic thought it 'a sweaty selection of the tales' whilst another highlighted the 'forest of male genitalia'. Hugh Griffith was superbly cast as Sir January, the old man who in The Merchant's Tale is struck blind, thus enabling his young wife to commit adultery before his very eyes. It now seems entirely appropriate that this Welsh actor should be associated with a venture that was intended to be a hymn of praise for European peasantry and which at the same time is cited in all the standard texts which trace the rise of sexual explicitness in contemporary cinema.

Quite rightly, Hugh Griffith's distinguished career was rewarded by honours bestowed in Wales. He was admitted to the Gorsedd and awarded a D.Litt. by the University of Wales. Of course the ageing bohemian was never quite as respectable as those occasions and other formal publicity would suggest. The man who loved corgis and restoring old property was even more fond of the bottle and there are marvellous stories of his drinking feats and his characteristic drinker's ruses. 'I'll stick to the water', he would tell guests as he served them a mid-morning lager whilst settling down with a full tumbler of vodka and turning to strike a match on the adjacent Oscar. We see something of this in the last glimpse of him that his public were to be afforded. In the BBC's film *Grand Slam*, directed by John Hefin, he plays the undertaker Caradog Lloyd Evans who on the rugby supporters' flight to Paris asks the stewardess for 'a large brandy', an order he revises to one of 'half-a-dozen miniatures' when the set-up is explained. At first his character looks suitably sepulchral, as we see only a pale raw face which is all bushy sideburns, eyebrows, popping eyes and fleshy lips but, as the brandy cuts in and the memories of his wartime affair in Paris are rekindled, some life and warmth comes into his features. Early on, too, we are thrilled by the terrific voice which we hear at one moment barking orders and the next softly recalling his 'Little Butterfly'.

*Grand Slam* represented an important milestone in the process whereby Welsh television identified new genres and audiences and certainly it served to bring Hugh Griffith to the attention of a younger generation. The film, however, belonged to Windsor Davies whose character Mog Jones was perfectly conceived and realized. Alongside such a classic rendering of the Valleys' idiom Hugh Griffith was clearly miscast and not surprisingly he faded from the story. Wales was slipping into a more domestic mode and the era of grandiloquent gesture and blood-curdling rhetoric was coming to an end. As we watch the character Caradog Lloyd Evans recall his 'Little Butterfly' and hum 'Plaisir d'Amour', we must remember that the actor was a great Falstaff who, having played Lear at Swansea's Grand Theatre, recalled it as his favourite role. What I would give to have seen his Lear.

# $K$enneth Griffith

In 1995, at a time when every day one was expecting a breakthrough Welsh film, Chris Monger's *The Englishman Who Went Up a Hill but Came Down a Mountain* was a great disappointment. Essentially it was a surprising throwback to the days of Ealing comedy but now the description 'gentle' was less appropriate than the term 'bland'. The whole thing was underwritten and miscast. There were, however, two great consolations. Mid Wales looked stunningly beautiful: it quite effortlessly stole the film. But there was also Kenneth Griffith as the Revd Jones, the local minister, and the only character who was given any real edge. In one marvellous moment the cartographer is explaining to the villagers how the reference points of other summits are used to determine the elevation of any one individual mountain. 'But who establishes the height of the original reference point?' is one man's reasonable enquiry. The ensuing silence is broken only by Griffith's definitive 'Well, God, of course'. Who could ever have doubted it?

It was wonderful to welcome back this old friend who, apart from a 1994 cameo in the hit comedy *Four Weddings and a Funeral*, had been away from the world of feature films for eight years. His memorable, incisive and much needed contribution to *The Englishman* was a reprise, for it was exactly the kind of work he had been doing for British directors several decades earlier. It was almost as if he was saying to Chris Monger and the new company of directors: 'I was the best thing in those old comedies; if that is what you want, then I will show you how good I was.'

What we think of as the Ealing format emerged out of the Second World War when in the interests of national unity it was assumed that any collective venture, whether heroic or comic, would involve a 'platoon' of characters which would inevitably include a Cockney smart-alec, a dour Scot and a chatty Welshman. The journalist Alan Watkins once memorably complained that it had seemed to him whilst growing up in Ammanford that all too often in action films the Welsh character was killed off in the first reel. Nevertheless, it was this war-inspired attempt at British inclusiveness which introduced a Welsh dimension into the film studios that encircle London and gave several actors trained in that Welsh tradition of theatre that had burgeoned in the 1930s and 1940s the chance of wider fame. Consequently, a Welsh cinematic repertory company had emerged and actors like Mervyn Johns, Clifford Evans, Donald Houston and Meredith Edwards earned a steady living either adding a Welsh role to an English tale or starring in that clutch of Welsh comedies that grew out of the metropolitan perception of Wales at that time. As British cinema attempted to broaden its social frame of reference it had resorted to music-hall stereotypes, a tendency which seemed to fit in with both the talents and inclinations of what were thought of as regional writers and actors. In this situation, it was very much up to individual actors to determine the degree to which they could inject an added dimension or some spice into the stereotype. It was precisely for this reason that the two Griffiths (and how often critics and commentators sloppily accorded each of them a final erroneous 's') stood out.

The extent to which Kenneth Griffith realized that it was up to him to seize the moment by giving edge to his scraps of dialogue is neatly, if somewhat unintentionally, revealed in his 1994 autobiography *The Fool's Pardon*. With obvious gratitude he recalls a moment during the shooting of *I'm All Right Jack*, a film which achieved notoriety as a result of its effective satire of trade unionism even as it gained enormous affection for allowing Peter Sellers to confirm his comic genius in the part of the shop steward Kite. Griffith plays Dai, a minor character who is just one of 'the platoon' of union agitators, somebody in the second row behind a selection of English character actors. His one significant moment comes when he, as a mealy-mouthed, boot-licking and, of course, Welsh sneak, has to report to the all-powerful Kite that newcomer Ian Carmichael is breaking all the union conventions by working too hard. After one take Peter Sellers spontaneously applauded this speech: 'Peter Sellers', reports Griffith, 'always treated me as a peer.'

In a 1997 conversation with Brian McFarlane, Griffith recalled his relationship with Richard Burton, a star actor who was actually four years his junior. When they had first met, Burton had struck Griffith as being 'extremely handsome, one of the most beautiful young men' he had ever seen. But they were never to be close, in part because Burton was 'stand-offish' and also because Griffith 'always avoided that bonhomie with fellow Welshmen, that sort of club'. He even had reason to believe that Burton had twice vetoed his participation in upcoming films. However, they did work together in a 1978 film, *The Wild Geese*, a story of British mercenaries shot in Africa. Clearly Griffith was grateful for the opportunity to play 'Witty', an ugly gay hospital porter who has a moment of glory by standing his ground as all others panic and gunning down the natives, crying: 'Come on, my beauties.' Even more, though, he was to appreciate the informal moment when Burton came up to him and explained that in the early days he had always been 'in awe' of his talent.

Of such moments had Griffith's cinematic career been constructed. It was almost as if he had shaped his cameos with the sound of audiences clapping and the ringing praise of his fellow-professionals in his ears. But equally there was always to be considerable gratitude for all those producers and colleagues who had helped him to develop and deepen his public persona, initially in the theatre and subsequently in the film studios. His first great hero had been Tyrone Guthrie with whom he worked first at the Liverpool Playhouse and then at the Old Vic. In 1946, however, he had rejected the opportunity to play Mercutio and generally to take over Alec Guinness's roles at the Old Vic in order to appear in a melodrama *The Shop at Sly Corner* at the St Martin's Theatre. He was briefly to return to the Old Vic, but Edward Percy's play had effectively determined his career for he was to repeat the part of the blackmailer in the film version which starred Oscar Homolka. He had been identified as a cinematic villain and that was to be his general role in the early 1950s and from time to time thereafter. In 1982 Terence Pettigrew identified the 1971 film *Revenge* as the high water mark of Griffith's screen career. He was cast as Seely, a shabby tramp who is thought to be a child-killer and rapist and who is captured by the parents of one of his supposed victims and subsequently trussed up and beaten. It turns out that Seely is innocent, but of course Griffith's task had been to create a convincing child molester and that he had done to perfection. He had, in his playing, effectively clinched the claustrophobic terror the film required. As Pettigrew rightly comments, he had given 'everyone associated with this grubby production an acting lesson to remember'. He had become Britain's answer to Peter Lorre, an actor he somewhat resembled. For Pettigrew he had become one of our 'better lower-order nasties', ideally suited to portraying 'stale-breath characters'. He was 'nervy, mean-minded, deceptively servile and sinister'. With 'the eyes of a stag run to ground' and 'the fawning rhetoric of a hot car dealer', nothing he did 'seemed of itself, entirely savoury'.

Given his increasing domestic responsibilities, a succession of wives and a number of children, Griffith was forced to take work where he could find it and he admitted to being 'a good hustler'. Much of this inevitable screen villainy was nevertheless tedious, and more satisfactory roles only came courtesy of Roy Boulting, another hero whom Griffith was 'to love'. He failed to land the part of Pinky in *Brighton Rock* but, having missed out on playing what could and perhaps should have been the most memorable of his villains, he went on to make eleven films for the Boulting brothers. Of Roy Boulting, Griffith was to say that his role had been 'to feed me, clothe me, educate me' and in general 'make sure that my head was always above the water'. Artistically what Boulting set out to do was to develop Griffith's comic potential by harnessing the eccentric, if not positively insane, intensity of his characters to the services of satire and situation comedy. In the popular memory Griffith's hitherto undistinguished villains were replaced by a succession of little men, whether they be soldiers, clerks, undertakers or clergymen, in a range of films sending up almost every aspect of British society.

Undoubtedly this new chapter in his career reached fruition with Sidney Gilliat's film *Only Two Can Play*, released in 1962. Dave Berry has quite rightly nominated this adaptation of Kingsley Amis's novel *That Uncertain Feeling* as 'undoubtedly the funniest of all Welsh screen comedies'. Once again the film is above all associated with the ability of Peter Sellers to immerse himself completely in the creation of a fictional persona. He is absolutely perfect as the frustrated Swansea librarian John Lewis wanting more out of life than that offered by his tedious job, the phoney local cultural scene and his lacklustre marriage. On this occasion Griffith's contribution to the film was far from negligible. For his monumental biography of Sellers, Roger Lewis talked to Griffith who revealed that for one thing he had helped Sellers perfect his Welsh accent. He had done this by introducing him to suitable Welsh types such as the poet John Ormond. Griffith's own instructions were passed on to Sellers during the daily car journey to Swansea from Porthcawl; unlike Mai Zetterling and the rest of the cast Sellers had refused to stay in Swansea's Grand Hotel: one look was enough to convince Sellers that he and Griffith should decamp along the coast. The tutor did his work well for the 'educated upper-working-class valleys Welshman' that Sellers created was not only good enough to please Kingsley Amis but apparently was convincing enough off-camera to fool the clientele of a Swansea restaurant.

The genius of Sellers ensured that Sidney Gilliat's film would work as an indictment of provincial society and cultural pretension, but meanwhile the sharp professionalism of Kenneth Griffith constituted much of the comedy. Griffith played the very Welsh Ieuan Jenkins, John Lewis's colleague at the library and rival for promotion. Jenkins is the classic small man, the embittered failure, overwhelmed by everyday problems such as a perpetually sick wife and the difficulty of getting to work on time. Sellers and Griffith are superb in tandem, neatly conveying all the personal and sexual frustration and sheer claustrophobia of routine office employment. As in so many roles, Griffith was again able to create those moments in which his frustration and anger are given an acidic edge whilst remaining deeply comic. His early morning appearances, his fanatic's walk with one arm swinging and the other stiffly inert provide the film's most memorable and effective punctuation.

*Only Two Can Play* remains a delight, and to this day tales are told of this enterprise that brought together in Swansea so many of the glitterati. Amis himself, as Roger Lewis noted, was 'a connoisseur of shits', and it is well worth recalling his observations on the two men who had brought to life his brace of librarians. In a letter he told Roger Lewis that Sellers had impressed him 'as one of the most self-satisfied shits' he had ever met, whilst in his *Memoirs* he remembered Griffith as 'a fine actor and nasty little subversive creep'. Surely, adds Lewis, mindful of the help Griffith had given him with his Sellers book, this was to confuse the man with the part of Jenkins.

And yet it was as 'a subversive creep' that film audiences would think of Griffith and obviously that is an image of which any actor, however regularly employed and paid, would tire. In casting terms such an image must inevitably be a cul-de-sac, and I can think of only Donald Pleasance who was able to use it as a basis for something approaching stardom. In any case, typecasting was bound to frustrate a man as intelligent and interesting as Kenneth Griffith. His autobiography must have surprised readers, for many new sides of the author were revealed. Early on there is one telling broadside: 'I'm buggered', he says, 'if I'll ever happily call my homeland Dyfed.' But, in most respects, the Tenby boyhood that we are offered was one of utter normality. His parents had moved away and he was brought up by grandparents. Nevertheless, it was a comfortable life; his grandfather was a builder and ran a car and there was talk of the family having aristocratic blood. The young boy developed a passion for his county (which 'reeks of history'), for rugby and, courtesy of Evelyn Ward, his teacher at Greenhill Grammar School, for English literature. It was Miss Ward who asked him to play the title role in *Richard of Bordeaux*, and so it was a little later as a sixteen-year-old visiting his mother in the east of England that he became a professional actor at the Cambridge Festival Theatre. It was a progression utterly lacking in angst, abnormal perhaps only in its smoothness. The fact that his first starring role was as the evil protagonist in Emlyn Williams's *Night Must Fall* was of obvious long-term significance, but off-stage good luck and good friends remained the norm. He studied at a London art school, acted again for Emlyn in *The Corn is Green*, survived several years (and one nasty flying accident) with the RAF and then began working with Guthrie in Liverpool and at the Old Vic. It was an almost charmed early life.

Throughout his book Griffith, as we have noted, is firm in praise of his heroes and deeply grateful for the friendship of those he admires. He is particularly effusive about the part played in his career by Peter O'Toole: he confessed that such was the friendship, help and example set by O'Toole that he possibly 'overwhelmed my life'. What he liked about him was his larger-than-life quality, his determination to live his own life and at the same time to thrill his audiences by giving them theatrical experiences they would never forget. This projection of himself would proceed regardless of the critics and all those producers and theatre managers who were determined to clip the wings of actors and who were in the process of metamorphosing 'my profession from big act painters to often little insipid water-colourists'. Griffith, it turns out, is a total romantic as far as the theatre is concerned. He loves the notion of the histrionic personality thrilling audiences with grand gestures as he or she aims for total emotional effect. His great contemporary heroes were O'Toole and Sir Donald Wolfit. He was horrified by the critical reaction to the former's *Macbeth*; and, when invited to join the National Theatre, Griffith declined on the grounds that they had not given employment to Wolfit. These great stars who were always prepared to risk all in their performances were seen by Griffith as the heirs to the great English tradition of romantic acting that had been established by Garrick, Kean, Macready and Irving. Personally he was always inspired by the example of Edmund Kean, about whom he was later to make a television documentary. What drew him to Kean were the stories of his years of failure: for eight years he had struggled with poverty and hunger, at one stage walking with his family to and from Swansea where he played both Hamlet and Richard III. His eventual success came by chance: he just happened to be on hand when there was an emergency request for a Shylock. Kean had embodied integrity; he had never respected the authorities and he had always gone on fighting.

Few actors have so explicitly proclaimed such enthusiasm for the heroic tradition in English theatre as Griffith, and what is so remarkable about his enthusiasm is that it was made manifest by a professional actor who did not himself belong to that tradition. Griffith makes a clear distinction between the vast majority of actors, including most great stars, who rely on their own personality and charisma which they hone with each successive performance, and that minority of character actors who essentially build each new role afresh. This latter category tended not to produce stars, although he identifies Paul Muni, Alec Guinness, Peter Sellers and Noel Willman as exceptions. It was also his belief that he belonged 'to this special band of brothers'. What we are being given is a passionate endorsement of a great theatrical tradition from which Griffith as an actor felt excluded. Here, then, are the roots of his disillusionment: that early charmed life had turned a little stale, and the need to earn cash had eclipsed the romantic vision. O'Toole was 'emulating Kean: I was not'. A failure to land a major role at the Old Vic and then a growing frustration with his television and film roles pointed to a need for a mid-life career change. What was required was nothing less than 'personal and professional salvation' and fortunately a solution and way out emerged.

In the light of these extensive autobiographical hints the great satisfaction derived by Kenneth Griffith from his second career as the maker and presenter of documentary films becomes very understandable. Here at last were the starring roles that had been denied him in his first career; no longer did he have to play subversive creeps. Now he could be a Kean or a Wolfit or even an O'Toole fighting his corner. In one fell swoop those petty theatrical impresarios had been out-manoeuvred. His new job was one for which he was well prepared and now many elements in his life began to come together. 'All my films are sermons', admitted Griffith who had grown up a Methodist and who well remembered the ministers of old developing the *hwyl* and using a variety of gestures, including that of turning their backs on their congregations so that they could suddenly swing around to drive home their points. In later years the actor had reflected on the sheer theatricality of those old preachers, something that had been reinforced for him by the fact that many of the sermons had been delivered in a language which he could not understand. At one level, then, his own subsequent sermonizing was a matter of style: he had merely borrowed the techniques displayed in the pulpits, albeit with an awareness of the psychological satisfaction such exercises offered to both ministers and audiences. But there was far more to his televised 'sermons' than technique, for like the preachers of old the man who was now to put together filmed sermons had a message to deliver.

Documentary film-making allowed Griffith to return to that great interest in history which had been nurtured in Pembrokeshire, and which was spectacularly revived when an old friend took him away from an Old Vic company tour in South Africa to show him the real country. A visit to Ladysmith and flights over Basutoland quite simply, said Griffith, 'changed the course of my life'. He started to research the history of the Boers and that led to his book on the siege of Ladysmith and to a number of television films that enthusiastically espoused the Boer cause. From the very start of his career the new historian was unashamedly committed to a point of view. Quite explicitly he was to make the point that, in his work, he was 'dishing out the word of History intermingled with the Word of God'. He was only interested in history if it allowed him to identify and then to advocate the clear difference between what was 'right' and what was 'wrong'.

What Kenneth Griffith had stumbled on was certainly far more than a new career. He had indeed found 'salvation', for in highlighting the wrongs of history he had been able to construct his own political philosophy, one that brought together a number of facets in his own personality. As he reflected on the avarice and aggression of British imperial policy in southern Africa, on the viciousness of the British presence in Ireland, and on the nature of the British Raj he more fully understood his own Welshness and the Welsh Nationalist case as advocated by 'the splendid' Saunders Lewis. At the same time he had become more fully aware of how the nature of English radicalism had been distorted. He found that he had little in common with the heavily union-dominated Labour movement and far more empathy with the older radical tradition of Tom Paine. 'I am', he admitted, 'an ingrained nonconformist puritan', and his first inclination had been to call his autobiography *Out of Step* because of his 'strong impulse not to join anything' and to be opposed to the consensus. All successful careers rely on the harnessing of personal energies, particularly those rooted in the personality, and clearly the richness and fullness of Griffith's career rested on the way in which he used one profession to come to terms with both his own strengths and weaknesses before developing a new career in which he could maximize his potential by drawing on what he knew about himself and what he took to be the core of his being. The character actor had developed a range of skills that could now be more effectively deployed in not merely outlining but in actually personifying and exemplifying a political philosophy based on a strongly defined individual conscience and integrity.

In his autobiography Griffith makes clear his gratitude to those television executives and directors such as Geraint Stanley Jones and John Hefin who have helped him in his not untroubled career as a film-maker. Meanwhile, the film historian Dave Berry has provided a detailed critique of what he calls 'Griffith's fiercely partisan documentaries and maverick talent'. Berry's assessment is absolutely spot-on for he contrasts the negative aspects of the films, the sometimes manic tub-thumping and visual flatness, with the undoubted power of a presenter who demands attention. Justifiably, Berry praises those films that concentrate on a particular hero (notably Paine and Kean) as being the most effective. He also points to the influence that Griffith's output had on Welsh television generally, for other historians such as Gwyn Alf Williams, Wynford Vaughan Thomas and Dai Smith were encouraged to perform lectures in front of the cameras. In his analysis Berry gently, but carefully, gives particular attention and praise to John Hefin's 1976 film *Bus to Bosworth* in which Griffith plays a Welsh history teacher attempting to achieve some objectivity in his classroom treatment of Henry Tudor. Quite subtly Berry is making the point that this gentle comedy illustrates that television companies could do more with history than merely leaving it to individual star presenters. This short television film displays the charm, complexity and sheer satisfaction of researching and debating history far more effectively than highly subjective one-voiced documentaries.

Ultimately Griffith's more ambitious films have failed because of their intense subjectivity. Of course, the shortcomings and ruthlessness of British imperialism needed to be explained and surely the time was ripe for the voice of the old traditions of both dissenting radicalism and Tory anarchism to be heard again. But those positive energies needed to be utilized in a more critical and rounded context. In Griffith, his Welsh Dissenter's hatred of Empire has been uncritically harnessed to a romantic identification with the colonial struggle, especially in Ireland, in a way that leaves no room for detailed analysis, judicious shading and careful judgement. And, all the while, there is the image of a passionate presenter walking towards the camera and flashing his eyes in a way that suggests any contradiction on the part of the viewer will be punished in the after-life. As a type he remains the kind of old-fashioned and black-clad preacher whose intensity has relegated him to an unfashionable and obscure church and who only emerges to play a minor and disturbing role at funerals of long-forgotten relatives. Clive James once commented that 'Kenneth can ask you the time in a way that makes you wonder how he would play Richard III' and the critic was quite certain that the 'spinning, joking, ducking and weaving' the actor resorted to as he delivered the sermon on the Mount in his programme on Christ was the only explanation of why Christianity made such a big impact.

Watching his film biography of Michael Collins, *Hang Out Your Brightest Colours*, which was suppressed for many years, it is difficult not to conclude that Griffith seemed personally to need the cause of Irish republicanism more than the vast majority of citizens in the Irish

Republic. The actor's formidable intellect and energy had finally given him starring roles, but those of us who appreciate both the complexity of history and the subtlety of the cinema can only regret that Kenneth Griffith ceased to be the disciple of Tyrone Guthrie and Roy Boulting. The man so brilliantly dubbed 'The Tenby Poisoner' by the writer Alun Richards was born to be a character actor and that touch of terror and acid that he contributed to so many comedies will have left a far more indelible memory than the sledgehammer he brings to history. In the autumn of 2001 the film and television community of Wales joyously assembled in Cardiff to celebrate Kenneth's eightieth birthday and to experience once more that familiar sharp and wicked intelligence that for almost half a century has made him nothing less than our national witch-doctor.

# *A*nthony Hopkins

The English-speaking culture is one that invites and anticipates great acting; in every era identifiable and acclaimed stars are required to reinterpret and sustain classic drama whilst at the same time providing the thrills that theatre audiences rate so highly. The tradition of awarding theatrical knighthoods had become, as was noted earlier, the clearest confirmation of how great actors are perceived as being crucial indicators of the well-being of the culture. At the start of the twenty-first century Anthony Hopkins, who was knighted in 1993, was undoubtedly the most acclaimed and best-known classical actor in the English-speaking world. His theatrical greatness had been established by a clutch of performances that critics had found to be as exciting and challenging as any in modern times. In New York he had starred in *Equus* (1974) and Pinter's *Old Times* (1984) and then in London he set *The Times* alight with David Hare's *Pravda* (1985), *King Lear* (1986) and David Henry Hwang's *M. Butterfly* (1989). Meanwhile the actor who had so excited audiences in Broadway and in the West End had made over ninety feature films, the most spectacularly successful of which was *The Silence of the Lambs*. His performance as Hannibal Lecter won him the Best Actor Oscar for 1991 but it did far more than that, for the character he had created, 'Hannibal the cannibal', was described as 'the most feared man in America'. Hopkins had brought to a spectacular crescendo a career in which classical credentials had been combined uniquely with a facility to offer not only American but global popular culture a new mythology and demonology.

The extent and nature of the actor's personal and unrivalled triumph was made evident at the millennium. In 1999 he starred in Julie Taymor's 'stunning, surreal and post-everything' *Titus*, a film version of Shakespeare's bloodiest play, the rarely performed *Titus Andronicus*. Critics loved this brave and bold adaptation in which 'black comedy goes hand in hand with blood-curdling violence' and, as Titus, Hopkins was described as 'mesmerising'. What particularly delighted serious critics was that Taymor had so brilliantly illustrated the 'timelessness' of Shakespeare and had done so in cinematic terms. In the process she had relied heavily on a great Shakespearean actor who could do full justice to his lines whilst veering between military authority and high camp. But even as Hopkins was giving pleasure to art-house audiences he had not forgotten his mass audience. Throughout the 1990s film-goers had wanted more of Hannibal Lecter. There was to be frustration at the length of time Thomas Harris had taken to write the sequel and then came the rumour that Hopkins was having serious misgivings about the ethics of portraying new manifestations of evil. It was with considerable relief that in May 2000 it was confirmed that *Hannibal* was in production and that Hopkins would be starring. The fact that several groups in Florence protested about the way in which 'violent and gory scenes' were being shot at famous landmarks in their city gave the new $54m film all the publicity it required. The whole world knew that Hannibal was on the way back. In the event, the film itself was an artistic disappointment. Hopkins seemed to think that more camp was called for and the glossy settings and the absence of Jodie Foster further weakened the impact.

The juxtaposition of *Titus* and *Hannibal*, not to mention Hopkins's total earnings, would suggest that the 62-year-old had finally achieved some kind of professional resolution of a duality that had run through and possibly plagued his long career. From the moment he arrived at the National Theatre in 1965 he had been identified as a potential superstar. Olivier was notoriously attuned to spotting the young men who would take up his mantle and clearly he enjoyed teasing tyros with all the mischievousness of a death-bed patriarch. In 1967 he was forced by illness to drop out of one of his greatest roles, that of Captain Edgar in Strindberg's *The Dance of Death*. His place was taken by someone described by Olivier as 'a new, young actor of exceptional promise'. Callan quotes Olivier's observation that Hopkins 'walked away with the part of Edgar like a cat with a mouse between its teeth'. As early as 1967 glory, fame, artistic power and the knighthood beckoned. But Hopkins himself had a slightly different agenda. After 1967 he was not seen at the National until 1971 and then, after returning for a couple of roles, he disappeared again until 1985. An enormous amount has been written about the complex personal and professional reasons for Hopkins's rejection of what was thought to be his rightful place at the forefront of British classical theatre, but essentially the actor had been clinging to boyhood ambitions. From his youngest days he had been fascinated by

Hollywood and its male stars; he had written to Bogart for his autograph, he went to see the cult films over and over again and he was soon known for his impersonations of Bogart, Brando, Dean and other heroes. In later days he would drive to see Bogie's old home in Hollywood just for the inspiration. More than any other British actor of his era he took his standards and his concept of stardom from the Hollywood masters. It was alongside Bogie, Cagney and Lancaster that he wanted to be judged. It took him thirty years, but he would eventually secure his own place in the only pantheon that he really respected.

Those thirty years had been far from easy. Acting is a profession requiring tremendous discipline, terrific application and the harnessing of a variety of psychological and physical energies. And yet it is a necessarily public activity which provides no hiding place. Actors are judged as individuals and yet they have to work as part of a team, accommodating themselves at every stage to the moods and egos of producers, directors and co-stars. And all the while there are the assessments of audiences and critics, as well as the gossip of columnists. This is the world in which Anthony Hopkins – who was by all accounts an insecure, introverted, lonely, reflective, unscholarly, serious and depressive adolescent – chose to make his mark. The point has often been made that a good deal of great acting relies on the transmission of energy and the discharging of pent-up emotion but, nevertheless, to sustain a career an individual actor needs to have developed layers of protection that enable the time spent working to be accommodated within some kind of normal life. Without that protection the profession can become a living hell. Only gradually did the surprising details emerge that allow us now to appreciate fully the anguish, dissatisfaction and frustration which plagued the middle decades of Anthony Hopkins's career. For most of us the only clues had been all that coming and going, that yo-yoing between theatre and cinema, between London and Los Angeles and between being British and American. It took his British (and especially his Welsh) public thirty years to realize how 'quintessentially American' he is. This was argued in a *Sunday Times* profile in 2000, the year in which Hopkins became an American citizen. The actor himself had always known that he was in reality American. He had tried the place once before; now he could embrace his spiritual home because he was wealthy, independent, disciplined and mature enough to enjoy it to the full. The point the *Sunday Times* was making was that Hopkins was entitled to his American stardom for in the authentic and time-honoured native manner he had passed through the Valley of Despair before finding salvation in his profession. Wales and London could not compete with this Hollywood scripting.

When Hopkins opted for American citizenship there was much public consternation in Wales. There was disappointment, anger and a degree of misguided over-reaction, with one Welsh Assembly member demanding that the actor be stripped of his freemanship of the borough of Port Talbot. His decision should have come as no surprise to anybody who had followed his personal and professional development closely. As his career took off in the 1990s considerable publicity had attended Sir Anthony's 'return' to Wales; his donation of £1m to the National Trust to help conserve Snowdonia, his involvement with Theatr Clwyd, the filming of *August* and his encouragement to young Welsh actors, had seemed to add up to the beginning of a new era for Welsh film and drama. A Wales that was itself moving towards a new political and cultural awareness was eager for a major figurehead, but in the case of Sir Anthony the nation had adopted a perspective that was far too short-sighted. The actor who had left Wales in 1957 had never attempted to disguise his Welshness – indeed throughout his professional career he was to draw deeply on it – but satisfaction and fulfilment had never been conceived in Welsh terms.

From the moment I became aware of Anthony Hopkins I wanted him to be acclaimed as a great actor and I was thrilled at the prospect of somebody who was so clearly a product of industrial south Wales achieving a place at the forefront of British theatre and cinema. I saw him first in the 1968 movie *The Lion in Winter*, a film I had warmly welcomed in my belief that film-makers had neglected British history to their cost. History offers great themes and our best actors were born to make their entrances as kings and queens. Here Peter O'Toole was repeating the role of King Henry II that he had played in *Becket*, but this time he had Katherine Hepburn as his queen in a James Goldman script that effectively combined the Middle Ages with utterly contemporary domestic squabbles. The film won three Oscars and the leading couple received deserved critical acclaim; Hopkins, playing Prince Richard, the son the queen wanted to be Henry's successor, made sure that all his scenes really counted. His prince was clearly gay, sensitive, refined, purposeful and determined. Many critics commented on how the appropriate settings had not been able to disguise the theatrical nature of the script, but what was more to the point was that the acting by O'Toole and Hopkins was British classical acting at its best and was being deployed effectively on film. I knew nothing about Hopkins and rushed from the cinema to do some research. I had immediately been put in mind of Richard Burton, not least because he had played opposite O'Toole in *Becket*; the assumption was that he had established a monopoly on any royal roles requiring Welsh accents. In time the differences between Port Talbot's two great sons were to become apparent, but on that first acquaintance with Hopkins it was the shared qualities that had registered. On film Hopkins had displayed a very real four-square presence and the voice had been gloriously and authentically south Walian whilst making every word count in the classic manner. At that time he still looked a little like Burton. They were to develop physically in different ways but there were many early photographs in which the curly-haired Hopkins could be Burton's double, particularly perhaps in his National Service shots. When I left the cinema after *The Lion in Winter* I was convinced that the whole triumphant early Burton phenomenon was to be reprised, and I was ready to lead the cheering.

I cheered Hopkins loudly too when I saw him next, which was in the BBC's *War and Peace* in 1972. In this massive eighteen-hour drama Hopkins played Pierre Bezuhov, a part for which he was to win the Society of Film and Television Arts best actor award. I suppose any young person who has read Tolstoy's novel has their own image of Pierre, a diffident romantic who somewhat blunders through romance and war as he comes to understand the truth of things. He is a hugely complex character who is made to pass through many different emotions and moods, but it seemed to me at the time that Hopkins got it exactly right. His difference from Burton had now become apparent for, here, Hopkins seemed entirely comfortable and natural as the portly, bespectacled, apologetic Pierre. Quentin Falk neatly summed up his appearance and demeanour as owlish and Pickwickian, and Clive James immediately spotted that the series was rather underwritten so that Hopkins had to rely 'valiantly' on a bemused giggle. On reflection, many of the mannered techniques that were to alienate later critics of his acting can be seen in this playing of Pierre, but at the time his diffidence, hesitancy and broken delivery seemed absolutely right. He was the ideal Pierre and he would have to be cast in any all-time ideal *War and Peace* production along with Audrey Hepburn's Natasha from the 1956 film and Sergei Bondarchuk's battle scenes from the 1967 Russian version. In his biography of Hopkins Michael Feeney Callan has indicated how much Hopkins related to this part. Quite apart from identifying with Pierre's mixture of gentleness and passion, Hopkins had researched the novel in full and was also able to draw on his childhood fascination with Russia which he had picked up from his grandfather. Fifteen years earlier when a student at Cardiff he had struck his tutor Raymond Edwards as being 'Chekhovian', and perhaps it was this opportunity in 1972 to play one of the great characters in Russian literature that allowed Hopkins to establish the formidable elements of his style. He has, in a sense, gone on playing Pierre in many subsequent films and television plays.

For me, Hopkins's Pierre had fully established his greatness and I eagerly awaited further triumphs. Disappointment was to follow in the years that followed, as his presence was noted in routine films in the cinema or on television. These were his dark years when the issues of his drinking, his marriage, his nationality and his identity had to be sorted out. All the details have been documented by Michael Feeney Callan, though perhaps the best record of his anguish was provided by his starring role in Jean-Paul Sartre's *Kean*, made for the BBC in 1978. Roger Lewis has argued that the play itself is flawed in that Sartre wanted to indicate that Edmond Kean was a failure whilst presenting a text that invites a great performance. Hopkins, says Lewis, shows us precisely what the great Kean was like: 'mad, bad, dangerous to know'. For Clive James, Hopkins turned in 'a more than passable Great Actor number' and 'seized the opportunity with both hands, threw it across the room, picked it up again, throttled it, wrestled it to the floor and knelt panting on its chest'. At the same time he starred in *Magic*, the story of the schizophrenic ventriloquist dominated by his dummy and impelled to murder. His playing of the troubled hero earned the actor a certain degree of notoriety – which was to do his career no harm in the long term – but at the time the critics were far from pleased. Pauline Kael thought him 'bewilderingly miscast' and highlighted his lack of range and any lightness of touch; he had just been 'gloomily withdrawn'. *Time Out*'s Martin Auty thought the whole thing 'a farrago': 'Hopkins starts over the top and roars even higher.'

It was in the 1980s that Hopkins resurrected his career by progressively appearing in roles that suggested that he was now a serious actor deliberately planning the confirmation of his status. With the 1980 movie *The Elephant Man* I felt as if I had been reintroduced to an old friend. Playing Frederick Treves, the doctor who saves and protects the freak John Merrick, Hopkins now looked older, sleeker and more distinguished; in a controlled and understated performance he radiated authority and sympathy. An *Othello* and Ibsen's *Little Eyolf* for the BBC sustained the impression of an actor very much in control not only of his roles but of his career generally. For most critics *The Bounty* of 1984 was one remake too many of the old seafaring saga, but there was general admiration for Hopkins as a very English and sympathetic Captain Bligh reflecting sadly on his inability to match the charm and warmth of Mel Gibson's Christian. If a kind of middle-aged melancholy had become the actor's stock-in-trade he was now investing his characters with real humanity and distinction. By this time there was a clear sense that he had totally mastered the medium and that directors would now be queuing up for him to bring into any venture that aura of authority and importance, thereby guaranteeing the whole thing some gravitas.

Thankfully, however, Hopkins did not rest on his cinematic laurels. Mercifully, he was now fit and confident enough to take his place on the English-speaking world's most important stage. As had been exactly the case with Richard Burton, his notorious rejection of London's West End had been an expression of his dislike for the whole ethos of a culture of 'luvvies' all too prepared to accept the domination of directors. But by 1985 London's National Theatre and Hopkins had realized how much they needed each other. David Hare and Howard Brenton were in desperate need of a star presence, not only to give life to the character Lambert Le Roux who was to dominate their new play *Pravda*, but also to attract audiences to the 1,200 seats in the cavernous Olivier Theatre at the National. The authors went after the man they regarded as 'the legendary missing figure of British Theatre' and, after initial doubts,

Hopkins accepted a part with which he would establish forever his standing at the National and in London generally. In the event his Lambert Le Roux was to be a sensation, perhaps the most vivid, memorable and debated theatrical characterization in the post-war history of British theatre. At that time the chattering classes were developing a fascination with the new media tycoons who were taking over the press and television and what Hopkins revealed in the character of Le Roux confirmed all their worst fears. Most critics agreed that the play itself was unremarkable but, nevertheless, it gave Hopkins the opportunity to create a living ogre, a totally immoral villain with a reptilian delight in destroying the values and confidence of all his employees. Audiences were chilled to the bone but also thrilled by the inexorable logic of an editor who knew that every person had their price, that all loyalties and traditions are worthless and that all news, comment and analysis is mere 'stuff', merchandise to be marketed. Several writers noted that this Le Roux was in essence a cartoon character, a gross caricature, but the pleasure lay in considering how Hopkins sustained his spell. The basic elements were his plain suit, his thin sleeked-back hair, and a piercing South African accent to which Hopkins added a malicious smile and what Andrew Rissik in the *Literary Review* called a 'casual insolence and elegant self-assurance'. His body language was marvellous; he would pace the stage with remorseless energy, suddenly swing round to confront other characters and pounce on lines 'with feline speed'; and then standing, hands deep into pockets, he would smirk. Quite simply, said Roger Lewis, this was 'the best Richard III since Laurence Olivier's'.

*Pravda*, says Rissik, elevated Hopkins 'to the status of national talking point'. This was a bonus that the National could not afford to let slip, and now of course it had to be Shakespeare and in particular the lead in David Hare's production of *King Lear*. This was to be the first *Lear* done by the National, and there can have been few productions of this immensely complex and challenging play that have been so painstakingly discussed and analysed in the national press. *Pravda* had been an instant success and its power was effortlessly sustained throughout its seven-month run. *Lear* was to take a lot more thought, and with so many journalists eager to talk to London's great new star, we were all able to share in the initial planning and subsequent development of this new venture. Throughout his career Hopkins had prided himself on the way in which he researched and prepared for the roles he was to play; out of that preparatory work his sense of each character would emerge and his instincts could take over. With *Lear* this was unusually difficult. The role is, of course, notoriously unplayable, with the actor having to take up the challenge of eleven scenes spaced out over three and a half hours, each requiring a very different range of emotions. Traditionally, Lears get some of it right but all too often during the performance as a whole something is lost, whether it be the poetry, the authority, the rage, the madness or even the sheer tragedy. What soon became generally known was that Hopkins was finding it difficult to summon up the necessary depth of feeling, perhaps because he was notoriously averse to the public expression of emotion. As the first night of *Lear* approached so Hopkins realized that ultimately he would have to draw on his own emotional resources. As he searched for the clue to Lear's inner torment he thought back five years to how disturbed and frightened his father had been as death approached. 'On stage', he told the *Sunday Times*'s Tim Rayment, 'I feel like my father as he looked in his last days.' In other interviews he explained that in generating anger he had fallen back on the image of his grandfather, Old Dick, a strong-headed socialist in his younger days. At other times Hopkins would mention his Victorian grandfather's frustration, harshness and rage in connection not only with Lambert Le Roux but also with Hitler whom Hopkins had played to some acclaim in *The Bunker*, an American TV movie made in 1980. Courtesy of the press, the elements that went into the assembly of this King Lear became common knowledge.

Remarkably, Hopkins was to play Lear one hundred times, a considerable physical and emotional feat. It was not a production that pleased the critics but it was always sold out; Hopkins was now that kind of star. As for his own performance, Irving Wardle in *The Times* thought it stupendous but overall the critics were divided and there were several references to the actor's restricted range, vocal limitations and 'inability to move the audience'. Hopkins himself was very dissatisfied and, convinced that the whole venture was not working, changed his emphasis, moving away from memories of Old Dick and relying more on his own internal anger and frustration.

Michael Feeney Callan has reported that his fellow actors were often aware that they were dealing with the rage of a former alcoholic. That rage frightened and indeed alienated some critics, but it was certainly something they all remembered. Jane Edwardes in *Time Out* thought Hopkins 'magnificent' and referred to his 'ferocious, primitive, bull-like' violence. It was very decidedly that rage which struck me most. This was not my favourite *Lear* although it offered many consolations. As always with this play, I was struck by how much it is an ensemble piece and not for the last time I came away treasuring memories of the scenes involving Gloucester, Kent and Edgar. Hopkins I had thought too young, too small, insufficiently regal and not lyrical enough to capture every aspect of Lear, but his anger was impressive and it dominated the Olivier. Furthermore, however much he was moving away from Old Dick, it was unmistakably a Welsh anger. As Lewis noted, 'some brand of Welsh patriarch rumbled in Lear' and at one level that was satisfying. It is always pleasing to come across familiar emotions and inflections in the theatre and on several occasions during the performance I thought of an old uncle of mine swearing at his sheepdogs. But surely, I immediately reflected, there are greater issues now at stake. I found myself thinking of Albert Finney's tribute to Donald Wolfit in *The Dresser* where there was a lot of ham in his playing of Lear but none the less that bellowing into the storm had something universal about it. At the National I had wanted Lear's intensity to have a wider range, to be just a little more histrionic.

I returned to the Olivier to see Hopkins in Peter Hall's production of *Antony and Cleopatra* and once again it was the actor's Welshness which was most striking and demanded analysis. The production was chiefly memorable for Judi Dench's wonderfully playful yet regal Cleopatra and Michael Bryant's exquisite delivery of Enobarbus's magnificent speeches. With such competition this Antony did not stand much of a chance, and once it was decided that the character would be depicted as a lush, as someone 'always in his cups', then there was to be little chance of a heroic note being struck. Milton Shulman was fascinated by this 'smouldering volcano of a man', whilst Michael Ratcliffe thought of Hopkins's Antony as 'an affectionate, exhausted and introspective old lion'. More than once during the evening I wondered if I was still watching scenes from *Lear*. Meanwhile there were times in the run when the writer Tirzah Lowen thought she was watching a version of *Who's Afraid of Virginia Woolf?* She recalled how, in rehearsal, Peter Hall had worried that Hopkins was exposing too much of his 'dark Welsh side', and indeed the actor himself had confessed to having much difficulty summoning up glamour. The scene of Antony and his colleagues carousing on board their ship came across as a night out on Port Talbot's waterfront, and whilst one could see that this 'pine was bark'd' there was little sense of an Antony ever having 'overtopp'd the world. I felt that I was watching a Welsh plebeian playing Antony and I spent the evening longing for Burton's patrician manner and polished delivery. It was two years later that I read Gerard Raymond's interview with Hopkins in *Theater Week* in which the actor explained how his theatrical performances were fired by an instability which resulted in 'huge surges of energy which come from nowhere' and often took the form of 'anger'. He spoke of how he charged into parts like Lear and Antony 'like somebody on fire' and speculated that 'maybe it is my Welsh background'; 'I create hell around me'. Later in the interview he admitted to sounding 'very peasant'; his verdict was that 'I am a Celtic peasant, very rough and very crude as an actor'.

Clearly there is a peasant, Old Dick side to Hopkins and it was fully exposed in his Shakespeare performances for the National. This aspect of his personality was very obviously looming large in his mind in 1989 and quite possibly his telling James Rampton that 'I am a Welsh peasant really. I have never got over that' could be explained by the fact that in that year he played the part of a Pembrokeshire farmer in a BBC Wales film *Heartland*. This first-ever genuinely Welsh role was well received, but during the shooting in the Preselis it was apparent that Hopkins had never previously been anywhere near a cow. He was on far more familiar ground when in that same year he starred in *A Chorus of Disapproval*, Michael Winner's film of the Alan Ayckbourn play. Now Hopkins was playing Dafydd Ap Llewellyn, an overwrought, small-town solicitor in the process of directing a local drama society's production of *Beggar's Opera*. Not surprisingly, Ayckbourn's depiction of amateur dramatics is hilariously accurate whilst, equally predictably, Michael Winner's treatment is way over the top. Even the producer admitted that the film, much of which was shot on location in Scarborough, was largely 'hammy'. Certainly Hopkins hams it up but in a totally convincing way. There is a wonderful bitter edge to this frustrated little stage Welshman who has a slight limp, wears a 'cardi' with a button missing and who alternates between battered suede shoes and bedroom slippers. 'Everything in this house was made in Wales', he explains to the very smooth Englishman who is new to the town, 'except the wife who was made in Middlesex.' This feisty, manipulative, pompous, sad and above all unfulfilled petit bourgeois was here being perfectly defined as a type, one who had walked straight out of the pages of the Welsh writer Alun Richards. In interviews Hopkins explained that the model for Dafydd had been his father, Young Dick, the Port Talbot baker with an arthritic knee and an obsession with work. I know of no interview in which the actor claimed to be 'a Welsh petit bourgeois', but that was the truth increasingly revealed in films such as *84 Charing Cross Road, Howards End, Shadowlands, The Remains of the Day* and of course *The Silence of the Lambs.*

The actor's petit-bourgeois upbringing is expertly traced in Michael Feeney Callan's biography with its emphasis on the loneliness of the only child, over-protective mothering, unhappy days at the boarding school at Cowbridge and the escape into the consolation of reading, the cinema and piano-playing. Fortunately, for a youngster with no talent for examinations or sport, Port Talbot offered one other possibility of fulfilment and so it was that the local YMCA Players acted as the conduit for the young Hopkins who was not particularly graceful but who nevertheless had blue eyes, a broad face, a good voice and an amazing talent for impersonations. These were the qualities that became apparent at the Welsh College of Music and Drama where he would begin the process of discovering what acting meant and, more significantly, what his life as a whole meant. Throughout the pages of this volume, appropriately subtitled 'In Darkness and Light', we can see the way in which Hopkins enriched his acting by drawing on the emotions of his upbringing as well as on the personal crisis and battles he had to endure. The subtitle suggests dualities between Wales and London, Britain and America, the screen and the stage, fulfilment and frustration, stability and depression. All the while, too, there has been a duality in the acting.

Always on tap was that bullishness to which many critics pointed in his great stage successes including the part of the French diplomat René

Gallimard in David Henry Hwang's play *M. Butterfly* which opened in London in 1989. Feeney Callan and other friends have rightly identified this role as representing the moment when Hopkins made absolutely clear his pre-eminent position as far as the London stage was concerned. He had chosen to play in his own inimitable way the part of a man unable to come to terms with the sexual ambiguity involved in his long-standing affair with a transvestite Peking opera singer. His interpretation surprised those critics who had seen a different cast on Broadway, but there was a general consensus that no other British actor could now generate so much powerful emotion on stage and express it so honestly and intelligently. Yet this naked display of emotional power was very different from his screen image in which he had continued to develop that Chekhovian control which Raymond Edwards had spotted in him when he was a student at Cardiff. Those Chekhovian mannerisms, which would become the basis of his film persona, are now as familiar to audiences as anything else in world cinema and they have attracted much hostile criticism. Falk notes that long ago Philip French spotted that Hopkins was becoming 'an irritatingly mannered' actor, a tendency which also irritated Pauline Kael who explained that on film 'Hopkins is Hopkins' and that he had taken over from Peter Finch as the face of 'middle-class suffering'. The worrying predictability of much of his screen acting was best summed up by his fellow National Theatre star Sir Robert Stephens in a piece on the career of Hugh Grant of whom he commented: 'It's not acting. It's a one-flick trick.' He then added that he felt the same about Hopkins, 'who had been hyphenating his words with naturalistic hums and hahs' ever since he played Chekhov at the Old Vic. 'He has all those stutters and scratches and coughs and mini splatters, it's always the same and it's awful. He's forever coughing and spitting and winking and blinking.' We have all had experience of this in many Hopkins films but we also know, as Stephens concedes, that the actor is far better than his mannerisms often suggest and the success of each role will depend on both the writing and his degree of control. The apologetic bumbling was perfect in *War and Peace* but later could seem all too much like the ingratiating deference of the corner shopkeeper. The reptilian dimension developed as Lambert Le Roux was more promising and it is that which triumphed in his totally controlled original Hannibal Lecter.

All those fluttering mannerisms are an essential part of the impersonator's armoury and it is his ability to do so many people and voices that makes Sir Anthony Hopkins such an accomplished entertainer. One felt that a *South Bank Show* in which he brilliantly brought alive Olivier, Burton and many of the stars of stage and screen could form the basis of one of the best one-man shows ever. His ability to impersonate partly explains why it is that, like Alec Guinness before him, he is called upon to play so many famous figures in history. His Hitler and Rabin were very effective, as was his starring role in Oliver Stone's *Nixon* where his physical differences from the former president were soon forgotten as a whole repertory of familiar gestures made that politician's demise all too intelligible. But his being asked to play famous men is more than a question of impersonation: it is also a question of natural authority. His fine head and resonant voice allowed him to step into history and it suggests that he has now replaced Jason Robards as the celluloid president par excellence as witnessed by his wonderful set-piece courtroom speech as John Quincy Adams in Steven Spielberg's *Amistad*. I suspect that there are many more presidents and world leaders to come. He was briefly Lloyd George in the 1972 film *Young Winston* and surely that is a characterization that needs to be reprised.

It was as much that general air of distinction as his acting success which accounted for the truly presidential reception that Hopkins received on his visits to Wales in the late 1980s and throughout the 1990s. With his University of Wales doctorate, his knighthood and his involvement with Snowdonia, Theatr Clwyd and young Welsh actors, it looked for a moment as though he was a political leader who had returned from exile to claim his country. It was a chapter which was bound to end in tears. The man who had so often firmly rejected Wales, London and the British stage knew exactly where he felt most at home. The bad feeling engendered by his well-paid adverts for a bank which was in the process of closing many of its Welsh branches and his opting for American citizenship were final confirmation of the fact that for some years Anthony Hopkins had been living in a republic which he truly wanted to claim as his own. Famously, in his drunken years, he had woken up in Phoenix, Arizona, with no idea of how he had got through the desert. That had been one of the moments of truth that led him in 1975 to Alcoholics Anonymous. It was also the beginning of that determined battle to control his acting and his life which allowed him to return to Los Angeles in 1995 knowing that he could enjoy the fruits of southern California on his own terms. The glory of his career is that professional and personal accomplishments have allowed him to lay claim to the adopted country which has fascinated him since youth. His friends now delight in his evident enjoyment of Santa Monica, Malibu and the wonderful desert hinterland. In quotation after quotation over the years he has explained that he does not need Wales; 'Wales', he once declared, 'is no solution.' That southern California has been a solution is an outcome for which we can join with Hopkins in giving thanks, although it must be said that a BBC television portrait of the actor made in 2002 as he prepared for his third outing as Hannibal was hugely disappointing for his admirers, revealing as it did a man with little respect for his theatrical triumphs, a man who quite clearly was working for the money.

A notion that has intrigued Roger Lewis and other writers is that Hopkins's return from the abyss and subsequent acclaim meant that he was now living out 'the career Richard Burton never had'. It seems remarkable that the two actors from Wales who made the greatest impact on the London stage and on the international cinema screen were both Port Talbot natives and yet had such little personal contact beyond the two brief encounters so often described. One would have thought that the two Welsh drinkers could have managed a few sessions together. For a while Hopkins had looked like Burton and, of course, he could do his voice and gestures at the drop of a hat, but the two men were very different. The miner's son never ceased to be an enthusiastic adolescent and yet he developed a patrician air; he was a king born to lead his men into battle, evoking the name of God as he did so. Meanwhile the baker's son, never really recovering from a lonely childhood, had been elected to the presidency of the republic, a man of temper but one also smooth enough to charm the voters: that casting as Nixon had been all too appropriate. Through their acting the two Port Talbot boys have taught the people of Wales many things about the dynamics of leadership, power and authority. They fascinate us not least because they are local boys; they were both unmistakably and irredeemably Welsh and as such both their lives and their work defined our own possibilities.

# $S$iân Phillips

Siân Phillips is the consummate professional of Welsh acting. Her own inherent theatricality made it inevitable that she would experience all the extremes that characterize 'luvviedom' and she has written of her 'roller-coaster life of much happiness and many troubles'. She has, however, survived, and has done so with her personality, integrity and values intact. In retrospect, it is not surprising that she has referred to her 'reasonableness' as her 'strongest resource', and it is surely this quality that has allowed her to weather crises that would have driven other sensitive souls into despair or addiction. At every crisis point Siân Phillips has managed to return to work, and success after success in a whole range of productions has always provided the reassurance that she is doing what she was born to do. Remarkably, she has combined a theatrical manner with a totally unaffected realization that she is merely a 'working actress'.

In a 2002 television profile Siân Phillips summed herself up as 'a Valleys girl with strong roots but with branches worldwide'. Those Welsh roots were lovingly described in *Private Faces*, a first volume of autobiography published in 1999. Readers who were enchanted by her account of a world in which 'everything was familiar and everything was marvellous' would have readily concluded that her reasonability and work ethic were acquired in the context of a Welsh family, chapel and grammar school. They may have been more surprised to learn that her acting and presentational skills were also developed in Wales. She was one of the discoveries of a new age of broadcasting, and her career as a teenager and undergraduate serves to remind us of how rich was the cultural life of Wales in the early 1950s. As much as any actor discussed in this volume she is the product of a distinctive Welsh culture, and her sheer professionalism should reassure us in our acceptance of theatre as a natural Welsh phenomenon. Inevitably, however, she left for RADA and a wider world: her professional work has been done very largely outside Wales. To this day her roles keep her in the West End or take her to Broadway and the West Coast, but she has often returned to Wales to be fêted, not least when launching her two volumes of autobiography. It is frustrating that we have not seen more of her theatre work in Wales, but at least she returns as a busy professional. In the time-honoured way, our inclination is to treat her as a personality, as a superstar, as a celebrity, but she refreshingly resists the candyfloss. When she comes to Wales she comes home. She is unmistakably 'one of us'. We take pride in her success and fame, but even more we should be thankful for her application, honesty and sense of perspective.

*Private Faces* opens with a map of the hills north of Pontardawe and the subsequent text and memorable photographs firmly establish that Siân Phillips was the product of a clearly defined world in which the predominant values were chiefly maintained by a matriarchy. We are left in no doubt that most of the actress's enduring qualities were inherited from ancestors who were the wives and daughters of hill farmers. She has taken her place in a formidable 'line of women'.

At the age of six, her grandmother took her to the pantomime at the Swansea Empire. As soon as the curtain went up the child knew that she was 'stage struck' and that she too had to be a performer. Home provided every incentive, for her schoolteacher mother directed children's plays and her policeman father was a singer, accompanist and choral conductor. In her local villages of Alltwen and then later Cwmllynfell there was a constant round of recitation and singing in schools, chapels and eisteddfodau. At Pontardawe Grammar School she was involved in 'the house choir, the gymnastic display group, the debating society, the Welsh society, the dramatic society, the French society, and the Youth Movement dance troupe'. At every point her qualities were noted and encouraged, and there was an increasing acceptance of the direction in which her career was developing. In her early teens she began to perform with the BBC repertory company in Cardiff and some of those plays were broadcast across the United Kingdom. When she was fifteen her mentors at the grammar school, S. G. Rees, the headteacher, and Eic Davies, the dramatist, arranged for her to perform scenes from *Twelfth Night* in front of the actor Hugh Griffith who recommended that she should think of trying for RADA. However, her talent had blossomed at such an early age that she had to wait a few further years in Wales. In Cardiff she studied English and philosophy at the university, acted and announced for the BBC and eventually joined an Arts Council Theatre Company which was being nurtured as an embryonic Welsh-speaking National Theatre. It was in 1955 that she finally arrived at RADA where, as an outstanding student, she won the distinguished Bancroft Prize.

In *Private Faces* there is a remarkable BBC photograph taken in 1958 which shows her rehearsing *Brad*, a play by Saunders Lewis which was being recorded in both English (as *Treason*) and Welsh. In the photograph, the eyes of Emlyn Williams, Siân herself, Meredith Edwards, Hugh David, Gareth Jones and Clifford Evans are all focused on the director Emyr Humphreys. Also in shot is Richard Burton who has closed his eyes as if contemplating some eternal verity. The image superbly reminds us that Welsh drama, so popular in the 1930s and 1940s, was now, courtesy of the BBC, achieving new glories in the 1950s. The involvement of so much talent in the bilingual presentation of a play by the nation's leading dramatist seemed to suggest a major cultural breakthrough. In the event that breakthrough never came, and all the formidable skills available on that day were to develop in different directions. Nevertheless, the photograph reminds us of the forces and energies that had brought all those actors, and perhaps Siân Phillips in particular, to the threshold of fame. In her autobiography she names the many talented directors, coaches and colleagues with whom it had been an exciting privilege to work in Cardiff. She had already made an impact in Chekhov and Ibsen, but at this time it was the work of Saunders Lewis with which she was particularly associated. In a sense she had become the cutting edge of his reputation as far as radio audiences and Welsh-speaking theatre-goers were concerned. In bringing alive plays such as *Blodeuwedd*, *Siwan* and *Brad*, she was repaying the playwright who had given her help and encouragement throughout her years in Wales. Saunders Lewis is very much the hero of the later chapters of *Private Faces*. By the opening of *Public Places*, her second volume of autobiography, a new guiding light has appeared in her career; and it did not take Peter O'Toole long to dismiss Lewis and to ensure that his wife joined him in a hectic international social round. For the moment Siân Phillips was in exile.

*Private Faces* was essentially a book about Wales. Necessarily, *Public Places* was concerned with O'Toole, both the living with him and the recovering from him. She is clear about her admiration for O'Toole; he was a new kind of actor bringing a revolutionary and déclassé charisma to the English stage. His progression from a strikingly original Shylock at Stratford to international superstardom in the film *Lawrence of Arabia* was, to her mind, thoroughly deserved. And, all the while, she was picking up professional tips; she claimed that she had learnt 'more about acting from O'Toole' than from any of her teachers. It was a glorious life: both husband and wife enjoyed café society, parties, 'wonderful sex' and the works of art they purchased for homes in Hampstead and Connemara and for their various temporary apartments. Given O'Toole's international fame and the birth of two daughters it was probably inevitable that her own career would suffer. But the truth was that O'Toole's increasingly narcissistic belief in his role as a Celtic man of destiny allowed little room for a rival talent. It emerged that he had little interest in promoting his wife's career. After twenty years the marriage collapsed and, with the help of a group of close friends and a third husband (there had been a short-lived union in the Cardiff days), she became once again a totally committed working actress, one who found new possibilities opening up.

Over the decades there must have been many children who, like the girl from Pontardawe, fell in love with the theatre at first sight. In time many of those with theatrical aspirations would fall by the wayside, some through lack of application, others through physical inadequacy. Few would have possessed a voice as well suited to the theatre as that of Siân Phillips. In fact her deeply appealing and somewhat throaty, if not catarrhal, voice is the product of hours of training by her mother, her teachers and instructors at RADA where her Welsh practices were particularly frowned upon. Naturally, hers were the providentially theatrical, and some would say patrician, cheekbones. A broad and well-structured face is a basic requirement for a stage actor, and certainly it was an open face, combined with her voice and her tall, slim physique and confident walk, which made her perfect for the intelligent, middle-class heroines which peopled those plays of Chekhov, Ibsen and Shaw that dominated the repertoire in the 1950s and 1960s. When I first saw her at the Vaudeville in 1966 playing opposite Alan Badel in Shaw's *Man and Superman* I was struck by the clarity of her diction in that wordy play, by the sheer joy of her acting and the confidence with which she claimed her space on the stage.

Clearly, Siân Phillips had all the physical requirements necessary for a career on the London stage. In terms of her undoubted beauty she was probably making her greatest impact at the very time she met O'Toole. His memorable judgement was that she was 'an estimable haughty bird, and beautiful in her younger days'. The photographs taken in the late 1950s when she had short dark hair certainly confirm her as one of the beauties of her day. She comments on the extent to which she resembled O'Toole. They had both made their West End debuts in *The Holiday* in which they played brother and sister, and in their early shots together there is a distinct sense of a shared narcissism. In time the photos reveal a somewhat gaunter aspect, and when the thin, straight hair is swept back a strikingly classic and regal head is exposed. The profile with its fine nose invites portrayal in sculptures, reliefs and, one is tempted to say, on postage stamps. In the photographic record of her visit to Angel Falls in Venezuela she offers a total contrast to the natives being, in her own words, 'androgynous, flat chested, wide shouldered, slim hipped, flat stomached'. What we see in these later images is the basic actress, the structure on which every role, courtesy of wigs and costumes, is to be built. It was not her beauty but her versatility that was to be the hallmark of her career. There was to be far more to her than the conventional leading roles of the early days had suggested.

Siân Phillips may have established her credentials in the West End but, as far as the nation as a whole was concerned, it was the 1976 television mini-series *I, Claudius* which made her a household name. The portents were not good. There was speculation that the BBC's limited resources and traditional costume-drama conventions were ill-suited for what was intended to be an epic tale of Roman emperors who regarded themselves as gods. Some critics were never to be convinced: Peter Buckman in *The Listener* thought it all a crude version of the Robert Graves books with 'the extraordinary wooden characters' providing 'no sense of doom only the manipulation of puppeteers' and 'cheap thrills'. The nation thought differently and soon responded to director Herbert Wise's strip-cartoon and soap-opera style of concentrating in close-ups on the machinations of the central plotters. Siân Phillips has explained how she soon got the hang of what was afoot and relaxed into the part. The series was exceptionally well cast but playing Livia, wife of Augustus, grandmother of Claudius and generally the power behind the throne, she stole the show in what historians of British television have described as 'a breathtaking performance'. Critics and viewers alike tuned in each week to check on Livia's dastardly deeds, all the while noting the realistic way in which the character was ageing. When she died in episode six the show lost a lot of its sparkle. Ian Hamilton in the *New Statesman* was greatly amused by the way in which Livia, having been 'poisoning her way through the series', nevertheless ended up making a request for deification which did not seem 'too presumptuous'. Meanwhile, on screen, Caligula, played by John Hurt, wished that she would 'stew in hell for ever and ever'.

Much television work followed in the aftermath of *I, Claudius*, notably in the John le Carré adaptations, but the machinations and the ageing of Livia had highlighted the impressive Phillips skull. Not surprisingly, Hollywood spotted her potential as an interplanetary exotic. Her shaven-headed role in David Lynch's *Dune* (1983) made her into one of the icons of sci-fi cinema, although the film itself was disappointing. Yet Siân Phillips's great gift was that she could avoid being typecast and she was still needed to play aristocrats and traditional heroines. Remarkably, the woman who had played Livia still had a good deal of the schoolgirl about her. It was often the case that her hairstyle or wigs gave her sophistication, but in interviews and photographs the natural fringe revealed a youthful innocence. In 2001 the *Western Mail*'s Liz Hoggard detected an 'almost childlike quality' in her playing in *Lettice and Lovage* in the West End.

Siân Phillips's essence as an actress became an issue on those unfortunately rare occasions when she returned to Wales to play women living in circumstances similar to those in which she had grown up. Immediately prior to *I, Claudius* she had played opposite a noticeably ill Stanley Baker in the BBC Wales production of *How Green Was My Valley*. At the time I did not enjoy this version of a story whose images from other times were already established in my mind. I did not feel part of the Morgan family as I had when reading the book and watching the two earlier filmed versions. In large part this was due to the stars playing the parents. I had instantly dismissed Siân as being too aristocratic and fashionable to play Beth Morgan, and I gave her no chance to redeem herself. The production is still not satisfactory, but I now feel myself enthralled by the sensitivity and vulnerability that she brought to the part. Quite rightly, the casting director challenged our assumptions; not every Welsh mam has to be played by Rachel Thomas. I am now very moved by the way in which Siân Phillips's very beautiful and elegant working-class mother is aged by the distress that comes to the family and the village. She was back in the Valleys in 1996 to play another mother, this time of a far more dysfunctional family, in Marc Evans's film of Ed Thomas's *House of America*. This time she was slumming it, whereas I wanted her to be playing a Welsh woman on her own terms, in essence to be herself, rather than lending herself to this bleak vision of a bastardized post-industrial south Wales. In my view, she was too interesting and sophisticated a person for the part.

For over twenty years now Siân Phillips's perceived sophistication has been accounted for above all by her successful career in musicals. Everyone assumes that this was a natural progression for a Valleys girl, but in 1980 when she agreed to play in *Pal Joey* she had to have her voice trained. Her decision to accept this challenge was probably the bravest and most important in her life. She had recently been divorced from O'Toole and she was gambling on a show that was to be presented in a converted Methodist chapel down the Mile End Road. She knew 'that she was on a hiding to nothing'. She was playing Vera, a wealthy married woman who falls for, and then promotes, a seedy nightclub entertainer. The *Spectator*'s Peter Jenkins reported that he had been waiting all his life to see a live production of this 'real McCoy of American musicals'. For this critic 'the world had stopped in 1940' and 'the hard-jazzy edge of the Rodgers and Hart music' had never been bettered. In the event he was delighted with the way in which the Half Moon Company 'lovingly and perfectly resurrected' the music. With her rendering of an 'unexpurgated' 'Bewitched, Bothered and Bewildered' she had 'stopped the show' and, given that she 'had no pretension to sing', Jenkins thought that was 'pretty damned terrific'. The *New Statesman*'s Christopher Edwards also believed that her rendering of this number was 'superb'. The show transferred to the West End and ran for over a year. Her career had been reborn; her life was once more based on a sure foundation.

It is probably inappropriate to talk of a late flowering of the career of someone who has always worked, but perhaps even the actress who bewitched critics in 1980 could not have predicted the successful career as a theatrical chanteuse that was to develop two decades later. Her decidedly sexy, undoubtedly gin-marinated and slightly world-weary baritone voice, was to grace a number of musicals, reviews and cabaret shows. In particular, she starred in Pam Gems's play *Marlene* depicting the life and singing of the legendary Marlene Dietrich. When Benedict Nightingale of *The Times* first saw the show in Oldham he had severe misgivings about the play itself, which was no more than a 'compendium', but 'at its core' there was a fine actress who had provided 'a star turn' playing Dietrich 'beautifully'. Of course, there was a striking physical resemblance between them, not least in the cheekbones and wide mouth, and the attempt at the Dietrichian vocal 'slur' was 'decent' and low enough. The show made it to London and, under the direction of Sean Mathias, was a big hit there and subsequently on Broadway.

In retrospect the London opening of *Marlene* will certainly be seen as the high point of Siân Phillips's long career. The *Independent* reported that she had been 'cheered to the rafters' and other reviewers were generous with their superlatives. For the *Observer* it was a 'sensational triumph for Siân Phillips', whilst the *Financial Times* nicely caught the general West End reaction when it announced that 'Dietrich rides again – splendidly'. Undoubtedly, the star of the show would have been most pleased by the comments of John Peter in the *Sunday Times*. Like many of us he had seen Dietrich herself perform, and his conclusion was that her new impersonator was 'even more perfect than the original', 'more perfect because Phillips, with great subtlety, adds the ingredient Dietrich wanted to hide: as the sinuous, silver *diseuse* performs her great songs, you sense the heartlessness which, unknown to Dietrich, gave her performance a slightly unpleasant, dangerous edge'. For Peter everything was right, the body movement, the fluttering hands, the voice and accent: Phillips was 'in total command'. He urged readers to go and enjoy this 'celebration', in which the star displayed 'regal confidence' in a 'superb, flawless impersonation'.

Approaching seventy and in her fifth decade as a professional performer, there is a pleasing and very appropriate duality in her public persona. In the wider world she is now known as a cabaret-style entertainer with her Dietrich, Sondheim and other numbers beautifully capturing the smoky, world-weary, bitter-sweet, reflective and sophisticated musings of exactly the kind of personality we imagine surviving a lifetime in that exotic nocturnal world of the city. Meanwhile when she comes home to Wales she is welcomed as Siân Phillips CBE, a grand figure of the classical theatre; this is the person that the University of Wales, the Welsh College of Music and Drama, the National Eisteddfod, Welsh BAFTA and the town of Pontardawe choose to honour. And quite rightly too, for as Liz Hoggard commented in her profile of the actress, 'she is fiercely patriotic'. More than any other Welsh actor she has taken the skills learnt and honed in a Welsh context and shown that they can be sustained and enhanced under the constant strains and pressures of the highest professional demands throughout the world. At every point, and not least after a long marriage in which she had been forced to make sacrifices, she has had to show both determination and flexibility in developing her quite considerable natural advantages. One relishes the way in which her recognizably south Wales persona has found a natural home, first in the classical theatre, and then in the *demi-monde* of musical review. We can all take pride in that stylish, confident stage presence and, even more, in that sexy and sophisticated posh Welsh voice. In her self she defines Welsh style and so is a key reference point in our cultural history. But as we reflect that she should have been the Welsh Olivier, the first person to lead our National Theatre – in which Saunders Lewis would have figured alongside Shaw and Ibsen – we realize that the world's gain has been our loss.

# *T*hree Welsh Hamlets

*In every actor is a Hamlet struggling to get out.* (Steven Berkoff)

Steven Berkoff's observation might or might not be valid, but what is certainly true is that every director of a new production of *Hamlet* wants his leading player not only to cast new light on the text but at the same time to create a Hamlet that strikes a contemporary note. In London and Stratford in particular the hope is always that the new production will produce a prince who, like Mark Rylance in 1989, is generally identified as 'the Hamlet of the era'.

Hamlet, famously, was 'sent into England' to recover his wits. 'If he do not', added the gravedigger, ''tis no great matter': ''twill not be seen in him there', for 'there the men are as mad as he'. Since the stunning impact of Richard Burton in the 1950s, three Welsh Hamlets have been 'sent into England' and their attempts to retain their wits have been very much noted by the natives. As it happens the three actors share what is essentially the same Welsh surname. They are Jonathan Pryce, Roger Rees and Paul Rhys.

## JONATHAN PRYCE

Jonathan Pryce played Hamlet at London's Royal Court Theatre in 1980. Since 1956 the English Stage Company had been attempting to revolutionize the national drama scene largely by producing new plays but now, in a change of tactic, they asked director Richard Eyre to breathe new life into the greatest play in the English language. The actor charged with this task was the Holywell-born Pryce, who had served a long and distinguished apprenticeship in provincial repertory. At the Liverpool Everyman he had starred in a production of *Richard III* in which Anthony Sher played Buckingham. Sher, who was later to be hailed as the best Richard of his era, recalled Pryce as 'a brilliant and dangerous actor' and 'a natural born Richard'. Under Alan Dosser's direction the actors had to perform as both acrobats and comedians within a set which formed a circus-like lions' cage. When told of the death of the young princes in the Tower this Richard had commented: 'Nice one Tyrrel.' In a sketch of the show Sher depicts Pryce hanging from the bars, part monkey and part Max Wall. However, it was in a Nottingham Playhouse production of a Trevor Griffiths play that Pryce was to make his breakthrough. *Comedians* transferred to the National Theatre in London and to New York, winning awards in both cities and establishing Pryce as one of the rising stars of the English theatre.

Griffiths was an avowedly militant socialist and *Comedians*, ostensibly a play about budding stand-up comedians, was a work which used music-hall conventions to examine both the impact of laughter on audiences and the possibility of revolutionary change. The many jokes dealt with what we would now call politically incorrect themes and explored the manner in which laughter could be engineered. Pryce played Gethin Price, a railway worker in real life and now the most promising student in an evening class for comedians. As the students prepare to perform in front of a London talent scout, Gethin develops what the critic Dominic Shellard described as 'a deliberately alienating routine' in which he appeared 'manic' and slightly terrifying. This Gethin was all aggression, a frustrated worker who came before us as a skinhead hooligan with even his hairy chest bristling with anger. It was a charismatic performance by Pryce and the critical acclaim ensured that awards would follow.

Pryce's Hamlet grew out of the energies he had released and the reputation he had secured in *Comedians*. Colin Ludlow identified the prevailing trait of this prince of Denmark as 'not melancholy but volatility'. This Hamlet was a tougher one than London was used to, and one that opened up many areas of debate. Here the prince's traditional indecision had been replaced by a 'nervous energy' that sustained the whole show. For Ludlow this Hamlet was 'by turns subdued, aggressive, witty, exultant, bitter. Coolly vicious in one scene, he is tender or scared in the next'. One significant virtue of this approach was that it established a 'much clearer insight into the meaning of Hamlet's behaviour to those around him'. In the *New Statesman* Benedict Nightingale spoke of Pryce's 'coiled menace' and of how face and body seemed to 'twitch, squirm and flail at will'; his whole being had become 'one agonised tic'.

Nightingale also noted that this Hamlet reacted particularly badly to the death of his father. The loss had 'pushed him to the border of madness'. One striking feature of the early part of this production was that the ghost of Hamlet's father had been dispensed with and his words were heard through the mouth of Hamlet himself. In fact these words were 'belched up' by Pryce in an 'agonised growl', for this Hamlet had indeed been possessed by his father's spirit. There were didactic critical complaints that some words were lost but this scene had a powerful impact. Years later Pryce explained how these moments had been shaped at the time by the impact of his own father's death which had followed a hammer attack by a teenager, a stroke and two years of disability. Not only had the actor had to live through that family trauma but subsequently there had been an occasion when, recalled Pryce, 'I thought I'd seen my father after he died'.

Many aspects of Eyre's *Hamlet* were hotly debated. The production's Ophelia, Harriet Walter, recalled that the director's eschewal of the supernatural and his emphasis on the politics was not to everyone's taste. That inveterate watcher of Hamlets, J. C. Trewin, thought that on this occasion the director had been far too obtrusive and as a consequence Jonathan Pryce 'had to bear with much'. Nevertheless, for Trewin this Hamlet had the merits of 'aspect, intensity and domination'. Nightingale did not like the overall production but admitted that in the title role there had been 'bravura stuff – like so much of Pryce'. James Fenton thought this a 'tremendous' *Hamlet* and noted how Pryce's 'Modigliani face' with its 'dominant brow' and 'the negative deceleration curve of his cheeks' took on a 'babyish quality' at times of suffering that was totally appropriate for the part. Richard Findlater, the historian of the English Stage Company, highlighted this as 'a landmark production', one that was a smash hit at the box office and at the same time 'hailed by some observers as the first definitive re-interpretation since David Warner in 1965'. Writing in 2001 David Thomas spoke of Pryce's Hamlet as 'one of the finest of its generation'.

The legacy of *Comedians* endured and in a variety of acclaimed roles Pryce sustained the notion that he was a dangerous performer. In Michael Bogdanov's production of *The Taming of the Shrew* the action opened with Pryce (as Sly/Petruchio) tearing down the set. On some evenings confused members of the audience attempted to restrain him and the police had to be sent for. However, he could also confound expectations and in so doing both surprise and please the critics. Irving Wardle much appreciated his 'gently affectionate Octavius' in *Antony and Cleopatra*, an intelligent reading of this normally cold-blooded character from an actor who was on other occasions 'electrically dangerous'. There was also a considerable degree of reinterpretation in a Stratford *Macbeth* in which Pryce starred with Sinead Cusack in 1986. His playing again generated 'alarm' and there were references to 'manic behaviour' and 'crazy psychic energy'. One critic noted his 'intelligent face and wounded eyes' but there was a general dislike of this 'hang-dog' Macbeth in whom jesting had replaced ambition and whose air of hopelessness could never have commanded loyalty or obedience. The value of the director's approach is best summed up in Michael Billington's judgement that these Macbeths constituted 'a Strindbergian couple locked together in love–hate', but we must set that alongside D. A. N. Jones's memorable verdict that what Pryce had come up with was 'a cheap little man trapped into some shoddy Scottish intrigue by a gang of fraudulent back-street spiritualists'.

In his comments on Pryce's career Anthony Sher noted the benefit that his friend had derived from being encouraged by one talented director, and in 1983 Richard Eyre again played an important part in keeping the Welsh actor in the public eye. *The Ploughman's Lunch* has become a cult classic and one of those films that is always referred to when the virtues and shortcomings of British national cinema are discussed. Eyre's film, written by Ian McEwan, focused on a BBC journalist James Penfield (Pryce) who, having commented on the manipulation of the media in eastern Europe, is writing a book on the Suez Crisis. In the course of the film we see Penfield pursue a wealthy girlfriend at the same time as he changes his anti-imperialist interpretation of Suez in the light of the euphoria occasioned by the Falklands War. The film was greeted as a timely critique of the British media, but both critics and public were alienated by the almost loving extent to which the film evoked the wine-bar world of the chattering classes. In America a movie tackling the issue of media manipulation would have become a smash hit, but *The Ploughman's Lunch* was destined to attract a low television audience and a limited art-house cinema distribution. It was too cool, too clever, too knowing and too literary. Ian McEwan admitted to the frustration of not being able to develop the psychology of film characters, whilst audiences would have regretted the lack of an identifiable hero, an error that Hollywood would never have made. Sheila Johnston brilliantly summed up Pryce's 'studiedly distanced performance', for his Penfield was 'a political chameleon with dead-eyed vacancy, soaking up and reproducing the colour around', 'a man without qualities'. All of this contributed greatly to what Richard Rayner described as 'the creeping accuracy' of the film, but it was not the stuff of box-office appeal. Pryce, however, had notched up a marker within the culture, and his soulless journalist was not forgotten. Fourteen years later he was to play Elliott Carver, the power-crazed media magnate, in *Tomorrow Never Dies* and in so doing offer the mass international audience which follows James Bond films one of that series's most memorable villains. The authors of *The Essential Bond* appreciated this 'cultured, intelligent and sarcastic' wife-killer in all his 'unabashed megalomania'. A new age, well versed in real-life media moguls, relished this entirely appropriate challenge to Bond.

By the time of his Bond adventure Pryce's career had taken off in a number of ways and he had become a truly international star. Initially he had resisted the lure of Hollywood, believing that his intensity as an actor worked best in the theatre and relishing his quiet family life in London. Undoubtedly, what is best described as the second half of his career began when his agent and various West End producers realized that he could sing. During his 'years of anger' he had kept quiet about his schoolboy solos at the eisteddfodau and his father's passion for crooning. Once the secret was out he was pitched into *Miss Saigon*, creating the role of the engineer, which he played first in London and then on Broadway where, having overcome permit difficulties, he won a Tony. Subsequently he played Fagin in a revival of *Oliver* and then Professor Higgins in a new production of *My Fair Lady* in which he won the admiration of London audiences not only by the way in which he coped with never knowing each evening who would be playing opposite him in the part of Eliza Dolittle, but also by genuinely singing the songs rather than speaking them in the Rex Harrison mode. Meanwhile the middle-aged Pryce was exuding authority and intelligence rather than anger, and one could see that, rather in the manner of Anthony Hopkins and Jason Robards, he was destined to play iconic roles within the culture. The key performances in this respect were his Lytton Strachey in the movie *Carrington* (1995) and his Perón opposite Madonna in *Evita* (1996). His television credentials were firmly established by the 1993 mini-series *Mr Wroe's Virgins* in which the strong feelings of the Victorian divine were beautifully conveyed by the camera's concentration on Pryce's large, brown and very emotional eyes.

One of the most gratifying aspects of this vastly distinguished, crowded and varied career is its recently acquired Welsh dimension. In both *The Testimony of Taliesin Jones* (1999) and *Very Annie Mary* (2000) Pryce played the father of unusually talented Welsh youngsters. It was the second of these films which aroused most discussion, for in Sara Sugarman's engaging film the actor was both attracted and surprised by the many similarities between the fictional Jack Pugh who was fascinated by Pavarotti and his own father who was much given to crooning 'I'll take you home again Kathleen'. In addition both fathers were to be incapacitated by massive strokes. The most memorable and daring moments in the film involve the heroine's unsentimental handling of her stricken father. This is black comedy of the highest order, and it is immensely pleasing to see Pryce responding so willingly to the originality of this film. The Flintshire actor obviously had no problems with the south Wales accent and the director, who was from north Wales, placed all her characters in valleys which have never been so beautifully photographed and in a zany story which faithfully reflects the comedy and frustrations of the post-industrial Wales of today.

In his visits to Wales Pryce has spoken of the trauma of the vicious incident that ruined his father's life, of his school adventures and of his pre-RADA days in which he contemplated careers in art and teaching. He has come to terms now with the passion that informed his early acting career. It has been warming to see his rediscovery of Welsh community and indeed the Welsh language itself which he spoke at the opening of the National Assembly for Wales. The *Spectator*'s critic Mark Steyn has recently made the perceptive observation that the versatile Pryce, with his providentially plain face, is the natural successor in the British theatrical world to the great Sir Alec Guinness. It is now exciting to contemplate all the many possibilities the availability of this great actor offers Welsh film-makers. Are we ready to confront anger, authority and intelligence in our own particular context?

## ROGER REES

Roger Rees, who is four years older than Jonathan Pryce, was born in Aberystwyth in 1944. His formative years were to be spent in London, where he was educated at Balham Secondary School and the Camberwell and Slade Schools of Art before making his professional debut at Wimbledon in 1964. As with Pryce, there was a significant and formative apprenticeship to be served before the dramatic breakthrough into the national consciousness. Pryce was to learn his trade in Liverpool, whereas Rees was essentially a product of the Royal Shakespeare Company which he joined in 1967. On trips to Stratford in the late 1960s and 1970s it was commonplace to see the tall, slim and elegant figure of Rees in the more important supporting roles. He would appear in his RSC guise at the Aldwych in London and in the company's many domestic and overseas tours. For a 1978 tour of twenty-six British towns led by Ian McKellen he devised a one-man show, *Is There Honey Still for Tea?*, described as 'an anthology entertainment about the English'. It was only after thirteen years of this stock work that his breakthrough came.

In 1980 the RSC staged an adaptation, by playwright David Edgar, of Charles Dickens's *The Life and Adventures of Nicholas Nickleby*. Dickens, of course, was a lover of the theatre and an actor manqué, whilst *Nicholas Nickleby* was a novel suffused in all things theatrical that had been both dramatized and staged in the author's lifetime. Nevertheless, the decision to proceed with the Edgar text (based on research by the co-directors Trevor Nunn and John Caird) was an incredibly brave one, for the production would last eight-and-a-half hours (not including intermissions) and involved a cast of forty-two playing 123 parts. In fact, the show was an enormous success both at London's Aldwych and on Broadway. It was acclaimed as one of the great theatrical events of the era, and one heard regular theatre-goers, many of whom returned to see it several times, describe it as the highlight of a lifetime. In the United Kingdom the BBC had developed a reputation for faithful adaptations of Dickens screened at Sunday teatime, but clearly the RSC had to find an extra dimension if they were to build an audience. The essence of the RSC's success was identified by the American critic Ethan Mordden when he spoke of how naturalism and realism in the acting had been combined with innovative and contemporary stagecraft. What thrilled audiences most was the ensemble acting and the way in which groups of characters would suddenly come together to create impressionistically all the atmosphere of a great Dickens set-piece. And according to Mordden, the action was 'centered' by the actor playing Nicholas Nickleby himself, Roger Rees.

Many critics have expressed dissatisfaction with the structure of *Nicholas Nickleby* in its original novel form. It worked better as a play, but it still required an effectively convincing depiction of the central character to hold together the bewildering alternation of good guys and bad guys and to give coherence to the successive crowd scenes. In fact the Dickens scholar Paul Schlicke thought that Roger Rees 'fleshed out the title role to an extent hard to imagine from Nicholas's presence on the page'. The actor's great problem was that of making interesting a character who was 'relentlessly nice', but in that task Benedict Nightingale thought that Rees 'coped well'. Mordden summed up this Nicholas as relying on 'hesitant and naïve but ultimately assertive good will'. Other critics referred to Rees's 'driving nervous zeal', his 'anger and poetic despair'. There was a general feeling that the show made considerably less impact when he was replaced in the part. Roger Lewis also mentioned Rees's hesitancy along with his petulance and jerkiness: 'rocking on his shoes', the actor resembled 'a colt'. Writing with hind-sight, Lewis reflected that Rees had 'suggested a Victorian Hamlet so much that when he played the Prince of Demark' he 'incarnated a proleptic Nickleby'. 'Nicholas', we are quite rightly reminded, 'like Hamlet, loves the theatre.'

Before playing the prince, Roger Rees was to secure his reputation as 'a man of the moment' by appearing in another play that concerned itself with the literary and intellectual role of theatre. Since the first performance of *Rosencrantz and Guildenstern are Dead* in 1966 Tom Stoppard had been writing plays that were highly entertaining and good box office even as they challenged audiences to think in a post-modern way about a number of dramatic conventions. His 1982 play *The Real Thing* was not to enter the popular imagination to the same extent as some of his earlier plays but it enjoyed a formidable critical success, both initially and when revived in 2001. As critic Robert Gordon was to explain, it was almost as if the playwright was responding to a challenge. His earlier plays had constituted wonderful and witty jokes;

but could he write a 'serious' commercial play about contemporary issues or, and this was the real critical challenge, personal feelings? Stoppard's response was a play that ingeniously uses the relationship of a married couple and the technique of plays within the play to examine the difficulty of writing about love. The central character Henry, a playwright, has difficulty in tackling the subject of love, 'the real thing'; of course, in depicting this dilemma, Stoppard himself writes a play about love. The critical reaction to this new development in Stoppard's output was best summed up by Benedict Nightingale in the *New Statesman* when he concluded that 'this is less a feely play about thinking people who feel than a thinky, a very thinky, play about feeling people who think'.

*The Real Thing* shared the London Critics Prize for Best New Play in 1982 and there was widespread admiration of Roger Rees's playing of Henry. The *Guardian*'s Michael Billington thought it 'a stunning performance, all nervous impulse and growing panic'. For Nightingale, Rees was 'an actor at once incisively interesting and marvellously unafraid of bold, sudden, un-English emotions'. Un-English or no, the casting of Rees was generally accepted as ideal: in his pullover, spectacles and beard he appeared every inch the British intellectual of that era. Robert Gordon noted that the reviews stressed the degree to which Rees and Felicity Kendal had created 'the illusion either that they were the characters or that the characters were them'. When the play opened in New York, Benedict Nightingale thought even more of it, not least because of nuances added by the new casting of Jeremy Irons who offered a more melancholic and ultimately defeated Henry. Nevertheless, he recalled with pleasure the volatility and wit of Rees, a more 'external' but none the less 'bravura performer'.

Since he had put critics in mind of Hamlet for years there was a degree of inevitability about Rees being asked to become Stratford's fiftieth Prince in 1984. Of course, the Nickleby persona was in everyone's mind. Michael Ratcliffe of *The Times* described how 'the moist eyes that widened with expectations of justice on earth in Nicholas Nickleby are here strained from sleeplessness and exhausted by the certainty that there is no hope from the start'. Ratcliffe explained that this was a colossal jump in Rees's career as he had never played a tragic role. He thought the playing would improve, but on first acquaintance he was not convinced by this evasive, quirky Hamlet whose voice trailed away. What had been offered were the 'mannerisms of a fine technician afraid to let go'. Reading the critics I cannot help feeling that in part Rees was paying the price for looking too much like everyone's stereotype of Hamlet, and the production photographs rather confirm that impression. This prince was 'haggard and hollow-eyed', an 'edgy young man – totally neurotic with eyes that flash countless messages of internal torment', 'a grief stricken whinger' and 'a developing psychopath – never far away from real twitching lunacy'. Christopher Edwards of the *New Statesman* thought it a coherent production but that Rees with his 'characteristically fretful energy' and 'sense of baulked manhood' had created 'a somewhat lightweight Hamlet'.

The production did have its supporters. In *The Times* Irving Wardle thought Rees had offered 'as convincing a portrait as I have seen of a noble nature in the grip of some obscure poison', and Richard Edmonds of the *Birmingham Post* felt that by the end of the evening the actor held 'the theatre in the palm of his hand'. Here, he continued, was 'a man cheated by the false humanism of the Renaissance' and this telling of the story richly extends one's understanding of the dimension of tragedy'. Michael Billington traced Rees through four stages of spiritual progress and, at the end, detected a 'beautiful stoic resignation'. One theme running through all the reviews is the failure of Rees to convey the humour in the part. However, in that same Stratford season, he was praised for his playing of the nobleman Berowne in *Love's Labour's Lost* and in particular for his 'deep gawky humour'. Peter McGarry found that 'away from his uneasy and posturing Hamlet', Rees had now fashioned a 'somewhat cynical playboy'. For Jack Tinker this Berowne 'wears his skittish cynicism as lightly as a paper hat at a birthday party', whilst for Christopher Edwards the character Rees was projecting was both 'sardonic' and 'compelling'.

Nobody is remembered for playing a compelling Berowne, nor particularly for 'a lightweight Hamlet'. But Roger Rees will always have the satisfaction of having starred in one of the greatest theatrical triumphs ever staged in London. For all time he will earn the gratitude of those who were thrilled to see the bringing alive of a central character in the work of the nation's best-loved novelist. Every actor may feel that he was born to play Hamlet but most would settle for having achieved a distinctive niche in the culture. As far as Hamlet was concerned, it was the fate of Roger Rees not to play the Hamlet of his era but rather to suggest that he could be precisely that. From 1980 on he was in effect playing Hamlet in the national mind. He was the culture's sensitive, scholarly, refined, gaunt and somewhat overwrought sixth-former and then undergraduate coming to terms with a brash world. His image leaps out from the photographic record of that era and it is not surprising that we have seen far less of him since then.

Regrettably, we saw him as a refined and sad sheriff of Rottingham in the Mel Brooks version of *Robin Hood* and knew that of all these *Men in Tights* Rees belonged elsewhere. It had been his fate physically to embody English youthful sensitivity at a particular moment, just adding that 'Celtic relish for inner turbulence' that Michael Billington detected in his Hamlet.

## PAUL RHYS

As the career of Roger Rees indicated, actors are both made and cursed by their physical appearance. When Paul Rhys won the Bancroft Gold Medal at RADA in 1986 (the last year in which it was awarded), there must have been many tutors and contemporaries who thought that here was another young man whose physical attributes suggested that he was destined to play Hamlet. When I first saw Rhys in Karl Francis's 1991 film *Rebecca's Daughters*, I adjudged him by far the best thing in a hopelessly misconceived venture and concluded that his Byronic playing of the young aristocrat associated with the rioters would lead on to other romantic heroes and, of course, inevitably to Hamlet. One could not help wondering whether in time Rhys would be another short-lived theatrical icon, a natural Hamlet with nowhere to go thereafter.

I first saw Rhys in the theatre in the Young Vic's 1996 production of one of my favourite plays, Eugene O'Neill's *Long Day's Journey into Night*. In this intense New England drama O'Neill was once again investigating his own family history and Rhys was cast as the younger and consumptive son Edmund Tyrone, clearly modelled on the author himself. This was a superb production played in the round, so that one was never sure which angle one would have on any particular family grouping. Richard Johnson and Penelope Wilton as the parents were both excellent, as was Rhys in his great scenes of confrontation with them. He was tall, thin, handsome and passionate, every inch the delicate and doomed oversensitive son. He held his corner in these intense domestic confrontations played out on the theatre's minuscule stage, and already it was easy to envisage the similar scenes with Gertrude and Ophelia that were bound to follow.

It was at the Young Vic in 1999 that Rhys was eventually to play Hamlet. This followed a busy few years in which he had combined the stage with movies such as *Vincent and Theo*, *Chaplin* and *Little Dorrit* and with regular employment in television drama, notably in *The Healer* for which he won the BAFTA (Wales) Award for Best Actor. His Hamlet was to divide the critics. Leading the attack was Benedict Nightingale who admitted that Rhys 'is undoubtedly one of our finest young actors' but felt that, as many actors had discovered, he was 'tackling a part that relentlessly exposes any holes in a performer's range'. For this critic there was far too much missing in this production. 'Where', he asked, 'is Hamlet's fire and frenzy', where his 'pride, vindictiveness, and ambition', where his 'soldier's eye', royalty and 'scathing humour'? In Rhys's interpretation of the prince as 'bereft but inadequate son' there was a 'sensitive intelligence and fastidious feeling', but all too often Nightingale was put in mind of the old hymn by a Hamlet who suggested a 'gentle Jesus meek and mild'. 'The hint of primness in his manner as well as Michael Howard in his vowels' was too much for this *Times* critic who in the last analysis thought Rhys's Hamlet 'a bit monstrous'.

A critical disagreement is one of the joys of the British press and it is remarkable how often the *Sunday Times* man seems to have seen a different play from his weekday colleague. John Peter thought this 'one of the most intelligent, thrilling and moving Hamlets' he had ever seen. He admired many aspects of Laurence Boswell's production which pulsated with 'intelligence and feeling' throughout. Paul Rhys's Hamlet was 'a Prince and an intellectual', with a 'tight little self-deprecating smile' and a 'vulnerability and diffidence that makes him so attractive to others'. This was an actor who understood 'the dynamics of inner crisis' and who revealed 'the ferocity of modern perceptions' whilst maintaining 'the iron control of the classical'.

Following Hamlet Paul Rhys did not disappear from view. Far from it, for he cropped up in almost every other television drama as he secured a reputation as one of the country's leading romantic heroes. His roles in dramas such as *The Cazalet Chronicle*, *The Innocent* and *I Saw You* were invariably accompanied by press profiles in which the actor went out of his way to emphasize that there was far more to him than had been suggested by the Japanese critic who, seeing him on tour, had described him as 'the Broody Dane'. Talking to Rob Driscoll, Rhys pointed out the irony of his 'posh image', whilst in his discussion with Heather Neill there was mention of 'the Toffs' such as Hamlet, Housman (in Stoppard's *Invention of Love*) and Edgar (in *Lear*) which he had played on the stage. What Rhys wanted the masses to know was that he was born in Neath in 1964, that he had a working-class upbringing in 'a tiny road of depressing houses', that his father was Welsh, his mother Irish, his uncle a boxer and his teachers the Catholic Brothers. The more assiduous readers would also learn that Rhys had broken his nose four times (once in rugby), that his first job was riding horses into the auction ring (another broken nose), that he fancied Anna Ford and that the three words he would use to describe himself were 'tall, Welsh and well-hung'. Who could ask for anything more?

By now the nation (including all casting directors) had the message that, for all his refined good looks, Paul Rhys is not a doomed aristocrat but rather a potential Hollywood heart-throb, a point of view eagerly sustained by American websites. Certainly it is fascinating to watch the actor increasing his range almost week by week, but I must admit to being not entirely convinced and to preferring my memories of the tortured toff. In recent years I have been thrilled most by his radio work and in particular his roles in Noel Coward's *The Vortex* and Ibsen's *Ghosts*, in both of which his frailty, anxiety and hopelessness were brilliantly conveyed by the providential break in his, yes, posh voice. His is one of the most distinctive and youthful voices in the land. We live in the era of new men and in British film Hugh Grant has determined most of the conventions. In her review of *I Saw You* the *Observer*'s Kathryn Flett spotted what was afoot. Flett could see that viewers were meant to want Fay Ripley (as Grace) to get back with Ben (Rhys) but she was not happy with this, for Ben was played by 'a Welsh Hugh Grant without the charisma, self-deprecating charm or the good lines'.

The clear implication here is that Rhys is being made to work against the grain, although one should note the personal slur, for Flett cannot refrain from drawing attention to the 'frankly mostly Welsh' actor. Not surprisingly, Rhys had also failed to impress A. A. Gill, 'principally because he seems to be constantly doing an imitation of Hugh Grant'.

We will see and read much more about Neath's Paul Rhys and we can only wish this attractive and talented actor well in his burgeoning career. He has confessed to 'a love-hate relationship with Wales' and clearly his future will be determined internationally. We can hope, too, that both he and his advisers realize that it is his intelligence and sensitivity which are his defining characteristics. He cannot go on playing Edmund Tyrone forever and there is plenty of time for him to go back to Hamlet and to many other classic roles for which he would be ideal. As his fortune accrues Rhys should reflect a little on who it was who wrote the best scripts he had to work with. Hugh Grant has yet to notch up a 'thrilling Hamlet'.

As the press profiles continued to appear I was delighted to hear that Rhys is to be relieved from playing Hugh Grant. The indications are that the actor has discovered Chekhov and that he is to play Ivanov at the National. If one follows Mark Steyn in seeing Jonathan Pryce as the new Guinness, then this latest news of Rhys enables us to think of him as a new Gielgud, whom I saw as a definitive Ivanov in the 1960s. The other news is that Rhys is also to play in *Woyzeck* at the Royal Court before filming it, possibly in Wales. Rhys has the talent, and more importantly the intelligence, to claim both the London stage and the art-house film sectors. As he returns to his natural pastures one senses that we will be reading even more about him in the years ahead.

The role of Hamlet continues to fascinate all those who work in or support English-language theatre. Hardly a year goes by without a leading director and aspiring actor announcing that a new production of the play is about to change all our thinking. In 2000 at Stratford I listened to a talk in which Simon Russell Beale, fresh from rehearsing the play, explained how the death of his own mother had informed his view of the role and how the experience was changing his view of himself. Every new Hamlet hopes to add an extra dimension to the part (and Russell Beale was certainly to do that), but what is most certain is that the actor concerned will learn many new things about himself. The three most recent Welsh Hamlets to grace the London stage were all made aware of both their strengths and their weaknesses. In the mirror that is Hamlet they learned precisely where they stood in the British theatrical culture. At the same time they had to confront their backgrounds for, as they played the greatest of English roles, they were made aware by the critics of how their Welshness had contributed anger, passion or inner turbulence. All the metropolitan reviews provide fascinating reading, for in the mirror that is Hamlet we learn not only about our actors but also about what those actors tell us about ourselves. Arguably, a culture produces the Hamlets it deserves. Meanwhile, a society should not be afraid to judge itself through what its actors reveal.

# *T*elevision's Repertory Company

In the second half of the twentieth century the United Kingdom relied on its national television service to sustain a political and cultural consensus. Foreign visitors were amused by the way in which, early each evening, well-spoken announcers would use the phrase 'your evening's viewing' to describe what was to be shown on the limited number of channels. To buy a television set was to join an extended family. The programmes were of a high standard, there was a balanced diet of comedy, light entertainment, current affairs and documentary, and there was widespread approval from the masses, critics and intellectuals, all of whom were anxious to maintain the one-nation consensus that had been the major legacy of the Second World War. The British had never been totally satisfied with their national cinema, which had always seemed an insipid version of Hollywood, but now it was widely accepted that television was a medium in which the country had found a legitimate form of national expression. And what was providentially crucial was that it was a medium controlled and regulated by the British themselves with democratically elected politicians having a major say in things. The tendency now was for British citizens to define themselves and identify their friends in terms of responses to programmes. Initially, identification was with favourite announcers and comedians and later with sit-coms and soap operas. To a degree that the old movie moguls could never have envisaged, all the classes and all the regions had come together to form a national audience.

The emergence of this national audience was to have enormous consequences in Wales. All the statistics relating to viewing figures, as well as those recording patterns of consumption and newspaper-readership, revealed that the people of Wales were an integral and unexceptional segment of the British population. In time, an important minority came to appreciate the dangers of this uniformity and began to campaign for a television service that would allow a fuller expression of Welsh cultural identity. The overwhelming concern of that minority was the fate of the Welsh language, but before looking at that story it is worth noting that, somewhat paradoxically, Wales as a whole was making far less impact on British culture in the age of television than it had in the age of cinema. Swamped as they had been by American and English movies, Welsh cinema audiences had become accustomed to spotting the odd Welsh star, the inevitable Welsh member of an army platoon and even an occasional Welsh film. Television seemed from the outset to be a very different matter, and we were to reduced to admiring the cultured tones of those personalities like Huw Wheldon and Wynford Vaughan Thomas who had established a professional broadcasting niche or to boasting of those actors or entertainers like Rupert Davies, Tommy Cooper, Petula Clark and Rolf Harris whose appearances in a programme would always lead to my father announcing that they were 'from Wales'. But in general we were not claiming our cultural space.

With a few honourable exceptions Welsh writers seemed unable to master the new idioms of television, and the sit-coms, drama series and costume dramas were not forthcoming. Inevitably, the successful television writers who did come out of Wales (people like Elaine Morgan, Alun Richards, Elwyn Jones and Ewart Alexander) were drawn into writing British rather than Welsh material. Not surprisingly, the rest of the United Kingdom rather lost interest in Wales and was quite content to go on thinking of it almost exclusively in terms of old music-hall stereotypes. Only now can we see that it was during these years that actors like William Squire and Hugh David and, particularly, Welsh-language actors such as John Ogwen and Stewart Jones were quietly developing a television tradition in Wales that served as a foundation for the more spectacular development that followed in the 1980s. Meanwhile, in the pre-1980s dispensation, it fell to a small number of highly distinctive and talented Welsh actors to represent their nation of Wales in the repertory company that now entertained Britain's huge national television audience.

For many decades one had the impression that the Valleys of south Wales were represented on British television almost exclusively by Glyn Houston, born in the Rhondda in 1925, the son of a Scottish footballer and a Welsh mother. Glyn was the younger brother of the handsome actor Donald Houston who had been spotted as a youth performing in the Llwynypia Boys' Club and given a starring role with Jean Simmons in the 1949 film *The Blue Lagoon* before becoming a very familiar figure in British films of the 1950s, including the very successful *Doctor in the*

*House.* In the 1960s Donald's career was to fade, and he became a recluse before eventually dying at his home in Portugal in 1991. Glyn was a very different kind of actor from Donald, who had always come across as the eager undergraduate type. The younger brother was unmistakably working class with a more rugged appearance that bore testimony to his having left school at thirteen and to his time spent working as a shunter in Cardiff docks and then doing military service, first in the wartime Fleet Air Arm and then with the army in India and the Far East. He first acted in the army's ENSA and then in rep before landing roles in films such as *The Blue Lamp* and *The Cruel Sea.* But it was as a television actor that he began to become the more familiar of the Houston faces. As he explained in an interview with Dean Powell of the *Western Mail,* his tough appearance and ability to do all the regional accents landed him steady employment in support or cameo roles in which he would play cops, villains, soldiers or working men. It was a time when most classically trained actors still avoided television, and in any case the new medium was attempting to achieve a greater realism and therefore welcomed actors from less orthodox backgrounds. Soon Glyn Houston's broken nose and slow, deliberate and slightly adenoidal tones became a familiar feature in stories with a contemporary theme. Most of Houston's work was placed in a British context, but he was also to play crucial roles in two excellent television dramas made in Wales. In Dennis Potter's *Where the Buffalo Roam,* he was superbly cast as the probation officer who was too set in his ways and too cautious to deal with the growing instability of the young offender whose passion for the Wild West is of a different order from that of middle-class intellectuals. Some twenty years later in *Better Days,* he played a retired miner forced to live with his socially ambitious son in Cardiff. The critic Dave Berry justly highlighted this award-winning performance and admired the way in which author Bob Pugh and director Alan Clayton brought the anti-Thatcher emphasis of the story to a climax by having the Houston character knock out his son, the short fuse being another of this actor's trade marks.

Since entering the acting profession Houston has lived close to London but, in recent years, he has returned to Wales to star in two further Welsh productions which confirm his authenticity as the personification of a significant era in our history. In the 1990s he put together as a one-man show a collection of the novelist Gwyn Thomas's stories which he then took on tour and recorded for HTV. He had appeared in the original production of Gwyn's play *The Keep* and had retained an affection for the writings of the Rhondda's greatest chronicler. Houston had mellowed with the years and it was clear that there was, as indeed there had always been, an element of reflection and irony in his playing. He had little of the novelist's theatricality, but he had all the dryness, edge and immaculate timing of a Thomas character. I sat in the theatre, closed my eyes and felt as if I were sitting on a bench in Meadow Prospect listening to the wisest of the local philosophers. Nobody has so definitively commemorated that instant and continuous commentary on all aspects of life that was such a joyous feature of Valleys life in the golden age. Houston returned to this mode for *A Light in the Valley*, Michael Bogdanov's film made for BBC Wales in 1999. Ultimately this kaleidoscopic view of the Rhondda's contemporary problems may have attempted too much, but at its core were the memories and troubled features of Glyn Houston's retired miner. In this actor the Rhondda of old lives on.

It is not far from Tonypandy to Merthyr Tydfil but, as the other familiar representative of the Valleys on national television, Philip Madoc was to convey very different qualities. Madoc, of course, will forever be associated with what the viewers of the new century voted television comedy's funniest-ever moment. In a 1973 episode (the only one in which he appeared) of the outstanding series *Dad's Army* he played a German U-boat captain who was detained by Captain Mainwaring's Home Guard platoon. Madoc warned his captors that after the war there would be reprisals. At this point the naive Pike insults the Germans: 'Vat is your name?', snarls Madoc. 'Don't tell him, Pike,' snaps Mainwaring. The Welsh actor will always be grateful for that moment gifted him by writers Jimmy Perry and David Croft. But it was not entirely fortuitous that he should be cast in such a part, for after Merthyr, where he was born in 1934, Madoc was educated first at Cardiff University, where he read German, French and classics, and then at the University of Vienna where he trained as an interpreter. In fact, he is an outstanding linguist who now speaks five languages in addition to the two he has known all his life. Travel remains his greatest passion, particularly backpacking in the Himalayas and Andes. 'He is a curious mix', concluded the *Western Mail*'s Hannah Jones, 'of Taffy boy done good and cosmopolitan gentleman.'

Philip Madoc has been British television's all-purpose foreigner. Directors have always known that they could depend not only on his accent and intelligence but also on the remarkable degree of authority conveyed by his solid build, his well-shaped head and above all his modulated bass voice. More often than not his foreigners, whether they are Germans, Italians, Russians, Jews or Mohicans, possess a certain rank or title. He is proud of having played both Lloyd George and Trotsky and is as much at home in a field marshal's uniform as he is wearing the insignias of the SS. But in Siân Trenberthy's superb portrait of him, taken in his dressing room at Stratford just before he went on stage to play the duke in *Measure for Measure*, his bearded look makes him every inch a European intellectual. One could easily believe that one was looking at a photograph of Sigmund Freud, a role that the actor should have played.

British television has long been characterized by a dependence on police dramas and, over the decades, every actor with a degree of authority and a temper has been called upon to play a part in the never-ending battle against dastardly villains. By the new century Madoc had become one of our longest serving officers. In the 1977 series *Target* he played Detective Chief Superintendent Tate in a regional crime squad series that starred Patrick Mower and was deliberately developed by the BBC as a rival to ITV's very successful *The Sweeney*. Both programmes were characterized by an emphasis on violence and bloodshed, and most critics felt that 'the comic-strip brutality' of *Target* was both unpleasant and unnecessary. In the second and final series of the show in 1978 the action was toned down in response to the complaints of viewers and watchdog organizations. By the 1990s, television executives in Wales were anxious that their channels should cash in on the passion for police programmes, aware that they represented a very convenient format for dealing dramatically with a wide range of contemporary issues. The result was *A Mind to Kill*, a one-off drama made in back-to-back Welsh and English versions by S4C and Yorkshire Television that led to several subsequent mini-series. In these films Madoc was cast as what Dave Berry has described as 'the world-weary' Detective Chief Inspector Noel Bain. Bain has had to operate in a highly competitive world and the fact that he was 'made for television' and not a literary detective has meant that the main character has not developed the charisma of television's other senior police officers. Directed by Peter Edwards, the programmes are well made and plotted and spotting the Welsh locations is great fun; but perhaps this is one detective too many. I have certain regrets that as he approaches seventy this very fine actor, who played Lloyd George so sonorously in BBC Wales's ambitious 1981 series, is now best known in his native land as a somewhat bland and detached policeman.

Philip Madoc secured his reputation initially by playing what a recent critic described as 'sombre or menacing roles', but I will choose to remember the qualities of intellect and refinement that the Trenberthy portrait reveals, as well as the charm and humour that characterize his interviews. In 2001 I listened to his performance as Prospero in BBC Radio 3's broadcast of *The Tempest* in which Catrin Rhys played Miranda. Rather like Richard Burton he was at his least convincing when interacting with other characters, but in his monologues he was beautifully paced and every phrase was given the right emphasis. This was a truly melancholic and reflective Prospero and we were listening to an intimate confession in an account of events that may well have constituted a dream. This was audio Shakespeare at its best. The verse was spoken by one of the great Welsh voices and one that should have been heard far more often in Welsh programmes and on Welsh stages. This, too, is a voice that speaks out of our history and embodies our values. It is the voice of the pulpit, and it is a reflection of the pre-occupations of British television drama that its challenging roles have been given to men in German or police uniforms rather than in clerical collars. There is an old-world charm to Philip Madoc (which may owe something to Vienna), but I see in him all the worldly wisdom, inner peace and understanding of the *parchs*, the ministers who guided our lives in an earlier dispensation and knew that the power of language was a gift not to be taken lightly. I was not surprised to see that he describes himself as both a Buddhist and a Welsh Nationalist. What is needed now are roles like that of Prospero that allow him to convey what life has taught him.

A handful of other actors make up the Welsh contingent in the British repertory company. During the time of their marriage Ruth and Philip

Madoc had appeared together in the Lloyd George series, but from 1980 the RADA-trained actress, who was born in Norwich but brought up in Llansamlet, started achieving fame in the comedy series *Hi-de-Hi*. The setting was a holiday camp, and of the characters created by Jimmy Perry and David Croft the most memorable was Ruth Madoc's chief yellowcoat Gladys Pugh. Ruth admitted that in the show her accent, her bossiness and her lovesickness were all based on women she remembered from her childhood in south Wales. In particular she based her crush on her boss, played by Simon Cadell, on memories of a post-war period when there had been an acute shortage of menfolk. Across the land one started to hear terrible impersonations of Gladys, whilst in Wales men from the Valleys cringed at memories of intimidating shop assistants and regrettable one-night stands in Porthcawl. More recently, she has returned to Wales to live and to display her sheer professionalism in *Jack of Hearts*.

Like Ruth Madoc, Windsor Davies was born in England (in his case Canning Town) and was to achieve fame in a comedy series scripted by Perry and Croft. Quite vital was that, apart from living in the Ogmore Valley, working as a miner, in a factory and as a teacher, Davies had completed National Service. In *It Ain't Half Hot Mum* he was to play Sergeant-Major Williams who had been given the thankless task of looking after an army concert party in wartime India. The show dealt in all the prejudices and sexual stereotypes of army life, but the comedy was sustained for over fifty episodes by the casual ineptitude of the platoon and the anger, frustration and petty-mindedness of the meticulously professional man in charge. In every show Davies's anger would visibly come to the boil and his control over his aspirates would collapse as he surveyed the behaviour of this 'bunch of pooftahs'. This was an entirely accurate depiction of the kind of Welsh braggadocio seen in many former soldiers, policemen, councillors and trade union officials, and I was delighted that it eventually led to the actor landing one of the great comic parts in the history of Welsh broadcasting. Playing Mog, Davies provides the backbone in John Hefin's 1978 film *Grand Slam*. Rumour has it that now every party of Welsh rugby fans to enter a Parisian strip joint looks for one of their number to expose his red vest and to conduct a rendition of 'Love Divine All Loves Excelling'. Building on the music-hall idiom, Windsor Davies developed what was perhaps the most vivid and accurately observed Welsh screen persona of the television age.

Victor Spinetti has been essentially a stage and film actor and he will always be associated with his appearances in the Beatles films and alongside Richard Burton in *The Taming of the Shrew*, but he has frequently been seen on television in dramas or chat shows. What was pleasing about his broadcast conversations was his unashamed pride in his Valleys upbringing. The boy from Cwm was shaped by the movies he saw in the Coliseum, by the characters he met in his father's fish and chip shop, by his membership of the Ebbw Vale Amateur Dramatic Society and by his student days at the College of Music and Drama in Cardiff. When he received a Tony Award for the stage version of *Oh! What a Lovely War*, he was praised for his moving words in Italian. He later explained that he had been speaking made-up Welsh. As much as anybody, this almost seventy-year-old actor who is still walking the boards best represents that strand of zany anarchism that has always characterized Valleys' life.

Perhaps no other contemporary Welsh actor has been so effective in all the modes of theatre, film and television as Hywel Bennett. Born in Garnant in the Amman Valley in 1944, Bennett moved to London and from his grammar school joined the National Youth Theatre with whom he worked for five years before winning a scholarship to RADA. It was in 1966 that the cherubic, baby-faced actor entered the national consciousness. In the film of Bill Naughton's *The Family Way* he was the young newly wed unable to consummate his marriage, not least because in their small Lancashire house he was surrounded by his bride's family. In the same year he starred in Dennis Potter's television play *Where the Buffalo Roam*, in which he played the young Swansea lad Willy, once a bed-wetter and stutterer and now a fantasist whose humiliation at school is bound to end in violence. In the rather tame (if charming) comedy and in Potter's remarkably prescient examination of the link between popular culture and violence, the new preoccupations of the era were announced and inevitably Bennett's boy-man became associated with them. He was the star of *The Virgin Soldiers*, the film of the Leslie Thomas story of young British troops losing their innocence in the Far East, and of *Loot*, the outrageous Joe Orton black comedy in which his playing of Hal suggested that he was born to play anarchically disrespectful youths. Age did not wither him, however, and it was in his mid-thirties that his television career took off. He had appeared regularly on television since a 1963 episode of *Doctor Who*, but his star quality in the medium was determined by cameo roles in Dennis Potter's *Pennies From Heaven* (1978) and in John le Carré's *Tinker, Tailor, Soldier, Spy* (1979) and then again in the 1979 new series by Thames Television, *Shelley*, in which he played the title role. Created by the writer Peter Tilbury, the character Shelley became one of the defining personalities of the 1980s and the enormously successful show ran to seventy-one episodes before coming to an end (with one four-year break) after its tenth season in 1992. Bennett was outstanding as the geography Ph.D. who initially appears as a 28-year-old and develops into a layabout as he realizes that he is over-qualified for every job he attempts and opposed to the bureaucratic lunacies of the age. The character was originally conceived as being 'uncommitted, amoral, apolitical, selfish and randy', and Hywel Bennett brought to the part what one critic described as 'a petulant pout' and the ability to 'fire off' the hilarious and sarcastic one-liners 'like nuclear missiles'. As Mark Lewisohn notes, the whole show was 'centered unmistakably on a single actor', and as the cynical 'and ever idle philosopher' Bennett was staking out his own territory as a decidedly metropolitan type. He had become one of television's great Londoners. As Shelley he had been described by many critics as a successor to Tony Hancock, and in other plays, notably those by Dennis Potter, he emerged as a more sinister London type wearing a sheepskin jacket and existing in a criminal twilight zone.

During his breaks from *Shelley* Bennett appeared in major roles on the London stage, including the National Theatre, and he also directed plays at several provincial theatres, including Cardiff's Sherman Theatre. However, his television days were not over. As an indulgent lifestyle, emotional stress and the ravages of time left their mark on that once cherubic face, so Bennett's potential for villainy increased. In 2000 he returned to Wales to steal the show in a BBC comedy thriller *Dirty Work* in which he played a corrupt Cardiff building contractor. In the *Sunday Telegraph* John Preston explained how difficult it is to bring off comedy thrillers but this was 'a masterful example of how these things should be done', not least because of the 'tremendous' and 'fantastic' playing of Bennett as the 'bellowing, over-enunciating maniac who was as sinister as he was funny'. That voice, so familiar from countless television adverts, now has a gravelly quality and this actor's power to disturb is yet further enhanced. Hywel Bennett is not only a great character actor, he is one of our great characters. He has lived through an era for us and we need to treasure him.

There were other Welsh faces on television. Harry Secombe was ubiquitous, never ceasing to exude Swansea charm. Angharad Rees graced many roles but will be chiefly remembered for putting up with the 'rags, dirt and nits' in the very popular drama series *Poldark* in which she played Demelza. Throughout the 1990s, Rhyl-born Nerys Hughes worried her way through many series of the BBC's Liverpool sit-com *The Liver Birds*. Nevertheless, the fact remains that Wales had clearly failed to claim its space on British television. One significant failure came in the form of the comedians Ryan Davies and Ronnie Williams who, although immensely popular in Wales, failed to cash in on their national exposure on BBC1. This was taken as evidence that the Welsh idiom did not travel well. In the view of Geraint Stanley Jones, however, the early death of Ryan robbed the United Kingdom generally of 'a potentially great comic actor'. The lack of a Welsh-based sit-com and drama series became a continuing reminder of how, in the era of *Dr Finlay's Casebook*, Wales was totally unfashionable as compared with Scotland. What was especially galling was that when a Welsh sit-com did emerge in the rather tame shape of *The Magnificent Evans* it was one in which that quintessentially Home Counties actor Ronnie Barker hammed it up as a Welsh photographer. Barker was pure music hall, but on other occasions it was noticeable that accomplished English actors like Ian Holm and John Stride had no difficulty in deploying convincing Welsh accents.

Thanks in particular to the work of the historian John Davies it is now generally appreciated that in the mid-twentieth century it was the BBC that had decisively maintained the sense of Wales as a nation. As the television age developed apace it became more and more apparent that Wales could only develop into a distinct political and cultural entity if television executives took up the challenge and developed programmes made in Wales that could be placed at the centre of the country's life. It was the launch of S4C in 1982 along with developments at BBC Wales and HTV which transformed the nature of Wales in the last two decades of the century. At every point the crucial political changes were driven by wider cultural changes, and in this process the emergence of film and even more so of television drama were of vital significance. The story of how producers and writers struggled to find the scripts and then the actors to flesh them out has been well told by Dave Berry in his monumental *Wales and Cinema*. An indigenous repertory company needed to be built up. The Welsh had to learn to play themselves. This was to be the great achievement of that period, as comedies, costume dramas, literary classics and contemporary stories were brought to the screen by a new generation of bilingual actors recruited from colleges, schools and the many local amateur dramatic societies. In this coming of age, actors had to transcend the received stereotypes as they learnt the demands of the new realism and permissiveness. In Wales the faces of Myfanwy Talog, John Ogwen, Iola Gregory, Dafydd Hywel and Sue Roderick became increasingly familiar. As yet, however, there was no significant breakthrough into the British dimension; for that we had to await the arrival of a new generation of young actors, including the so-called Taff Pack.

In that flowering of Welsh film drama two performances did earn a degree of wider comment. One of the most exciting aspects of the period was the emergence of Karl Francis as a major director; his hallmark was his terrifically sensitive handling of both amateur and professional actors. In his *Boy Soldier* (also filmed in Welsh as *Milwr Bychan*) the Rhydfelen-educated Richard Lynch was extremely effective as the young Welsh soldier whose background makes him more sympathetic to the Irish nationalist cause than to his colleagues. In complete contrast the Andrew Davies adaptation of Kingsley Amis's *The Old Devils* offered a feast of fine acting in which honours went to a very ill Ray Smith. In his pomp, this actor had played a convincing Nye Bevan. Now, in what was to be his last role, he turned up as Charlie, the ageing philosopher and cynic who, as he drinks, is able to pour scorn on all the preoccupations of the arty-farty set of pseudo-intellectuals setting the local cultural tone. This veteran of the repertory company had ended his career in a grandstanding performance.

# *T*he Taff Pack

The state of Welsh cultural life at the millennium was perfectly exposed by the ease with which a group of talented young Welsh actors was identified as 'the Taff Pack'. The paperback edition of Shawn Levy's account of the original 'Rat Pack' with its cover picture of Sinatra and his mates in Las Vegas encouraged us to think of the five or so young Welshmen having a riotous evening in Malibu as they watched Wales play rugby on a big screen. In the Wales of that time there was little analysis of those educational developments that had allowed good-looking, talented and charming students to pass so quickly into British, and indeed international, attention. Even more perturbing was the absence of any debate as to the cultural implications of the sudden availability of this pool of acting talent. Evidently, their work and their artistic potential were less interesting than their fame. What seemed to matter most was that Wales had been given a new assortment of personalities.

The Taff Pack (or the *Taff Pac* as they were identified in Joanna Davies's cautionary study published in 2000) were quite simply the latest, and possibly the last, manifestation of 'Cool Cymru', that attempt by the media to suggest that the coming of the National Assembly had coincided with a flowering of contemporary youth culture and styles that had at last allowed Wales to escape from the stranglehold of well-worn stereotypes. The essential ingredient in the Cool Cymru scenario had been the phenomenal and deserved success in the 1990s of Welsh bands such as Catatonia and the Stereophonics, but what sustained the buzz was the way in which the Cardiff scene was now dominated by a new generation of bilingual young people, many of whom worked in the culture and entertainment industries. Even whimsical developments such as the emergence of the actor Stifyn Parr's group SWS (Social, Welsh and Sexy) indicated the desire of this initially London and later downtown Cardiff set to be accepted as being sophisticated and utterly contemporary, both in their own city and when on gigs in London or New York. The new energies and aspirations were real enough, and musically there was real distinction, but all the time mythology was racing ahead of analysis, not least because of the increasing tabloid hunger for gossip, celebrities and icons of what was identified as 'a new Wales'. There were now acres of column inches to be filled, and all the evidence suggested that youth was tired of Richard Burton and Shirley Bassey images and stories. The need was for beautiful people, groomed in Wales, proud to be Welsh and yet acclaimed worldwide.

For the actors who were to be eagerly taken up by the journalistic priests of Cool Cymru, Wales had undoubtedly been an inspiration. They were the products of the schools and television studios that had allowed the flowering of popular culture in the Wales of the 1990s. Nevertheless, their status as major stars had to be established by hard work and by passing all the vital tests in England. Undoubtedly, the most thrilling privilege afforded by the era was to be present at those performances in which individual Welsh actors first caught the eye of the London and Stratford critics.

What I came to identify as a new era for Welsh actors began for me at Stratford in 1994 when I saw Daniel Evans play the boy in *Henry V*. This was a powerful and effective production of a notoriously difficult play in which there has to be a balance between the personal and the jingoistic. It was a strong cast, and the fact that many of them were Celts nicely sustained one of the main themes. In what is Shakespeare's most Welsh play Fluellen was played by Linal Haft, a superb English character actor, but the necessary Welsh dimension was injected by Daniel Evans's very positive and determined boy who displayed a real authority in reporting Falstaff's death and subsequently rejecting the villainy of those 'three swashers', Nym, Pistol and Bardolph, who had been the great man's hangers-on. The brightness and clarity of this boy sent me straight to the programme where I learned that Evans had been born at 'Cwmparc, Y Rhondda'. Stratford programmes are rarely that precise. It was no surprise to read that in 1990 he had won 'the Richard Burton Award'.

I subsequently looked out for appearances of the boy from Cwmparc and my reward was two of the best evenings I have ever spent in the theatre. In the RSC's 1995 production of *A Midsummer Night's Dream* Evans was cast as Francis Flute and alongside him in the part of Bottom was another Welsh actor, Desmond Barrit. After a long career in provincial repertory the Port Talbot-born Barrit had emerged in the

1990s as one of London and Stratford's best classical comedy actors with his great breakthrough coming in the RSC's hilarious, slick and much acclaimed 1990 production of *The Comedy of Errors* in which he was cast as the twins Antipholus of Syracuse and Antipholus of Ephesus. My chief memory of that production was of Barrit's bulky silhouette gliding across the stage in one guise or other; deservedly he had won the Olivier Award for the Best Comedy Actor. Now, as Flute and Bottom, the two south Wales actors produced what I suggest must have been one of the funniest-ever versions of Shakespeare's most amusing scene, the play within the play, *The Tragedy of Pyramus and Thisbe*. It was done in classic Welsh camp and when Flute (as Thisbe) mourns the death of Pyramus and recalls, in a tone only previously heard in certain Cardiff pubs, that 'his eyes were green as leeks', my laughter prompted some to ask whether there was a doctor in the house. Charles Spencer in the *Daily Telegraph* thought Daniel 'utterly beguiling as Flute, a sly young adolescent who suddenly discovers he rather enjoys dressing up as a girl'. Barrit, described by Richard Edmonds as 'an actor who instantly lifts the spirits of the house', was of the wrong vintage to be taken up as a symbol of Cool Cymru but by the millennium he was undoubtedly one of the country's finest actors. His RSC Falstaff was acclaimed in London and Stratford. As the fat knight he was humorous but also deeply moving, a patriarch not without style, dignity, pathos or self-understanding. For Ian Johns of *The Times* it was 'a wonderfully unsentimental performance', whilst for the *Daily Telegraph*'s Charles Spencer Barrit was 'the Falstaff of one's dreams'.

In 1997 an event occurred that one instinctively knew would represent a high water mark in the history of Welsh theatre. *Cardiff East*, a play written and directed by the Cardiff-born Peter Gill, opened at the National Theatre in London. Almost certainly it was the fact that Gill had long been an associate director at the National that ensured that this play, set in the working-class suburbs of Cardiff, would open at the Cottesloe. It was also clear that an earlier production at the National of *Under Milk Wood* had created a taste for the Welsh idiom. From the start it was obvious that the *Cardiff East* evening would be a memorable one. The audience consisted almost entirely of Welsh friends living in exile, and their appetites were nicely whetted by a programme bristling with literary references to Cardiff and providing a veritable Who's Who of the Welsh acting profession. The veterans Windsor Davies and Gwenllian Davies were in the cast, presumably to keep an eye on the new generation represented by Lisa Palfrey, Di Botcher, Mark Lewis Jones and Andrew Howard. At the Cottesloe the play was staged almost as in a rehearsal room, and the cast of sixteen left their chairs to act out a virtual soap opera around the central character, the morose and philosophical Michael played by Kenneth Cranham. Michael has a story to tell and it is that which forms the play's centrepiece. It was difficult, though, not to be diverted by the natural enthusiasm and commitment of the younger members of the cast. Above all there was the friendship of the two young lads, Neil and Tommy, played by Daniel Evans and Matthew Rhys. In their relish for their roles they conveyed all the energy and enthusiasm of a new generation of Welsh youth and, in the scene when they strip and jump into bed with each other, the sense of a wind of change blowing through a society was quite palpable. That evening the play was intriguing, the young cast totally charming and the cultural portents thrilling.

Clearly, West End fame beckoned for these two attractive and talented actors. Daniel, a product of Ysgol Rhydfelen and the Guildhall School of Music and Drama, has been glimpsed in various television dramas but he seems to be happiest in live theatre. He is, perhaps, the most purely theatrical of all Welsh actors, most at home in make-up and wigs, a natural Puck with a wicked twinkle in his eyes, a born and effervescent entertainer. Most recently his biggest successes have come in musicals; he was memorable in the title role of the National's big hit *Candide* and in 2001 he won the Olivier for the Best Musical Actor for his playing in Stephen Sondheim's *Merrily We Roll Along*. He has in addition been critically acclaimed for his depiction of American gays in challenging new plays by Christopher Shinn staged at the Royal Court. In his review of *Where Do We Live* Benedict Nightingale referred to 'the excellent Evans'. The actor has declared an interest in performing in classical theatre in Wales, and it is not difficult to envisage him as one of the main attractions in both Welsh- and English-language productions on the stage of Cardiff's new Millennium Centre.

*Cardiff East* was Matthew Rhys's professional stage debut and had come three years after the Cardiff-born actor entered RADA and been the first recipient of the Lady Rothermere Award for the best drama student in the country. Just three years after *Cardiff East* he was chosen to play opposite the American star Kathleen Turner in a stage version of the 1960s film *The Graduate* in which Dustin Hoffman had made his name. The fact that Miss Turner would be briefly naked ensured that *The Graduate* became the hottest ticket in town and that, for a time, Rhys would become the most widely and extensively profiled actor in the country. In general the critics liked his playing of the highly anxious, frustrated and angry Ben who is seduced by the older woman. The profilers wanted to know all about those scenes, but there was also considerable fascination with the character whom Rhys was playing at that time in the television series *Metropolis*. On television Rhys was cast as a dope-smoking lout who was nevertheless sexually irresistible. Inevitably, the young actor was presented very much as a sex symbol in the national press, and there were extensive descriptions of his 'thick dark hair and pale blue eyes'. Then there would be a reference to 'his Welsh lilt' with comparisons made with the various Yorkshire, Cockney, Scouse and Californian accents which he had come up with in his recent film, television and stage work. And so the journalists moved quickly on to the matter of Rhys's Welshness.

'The first and most striking thing about Matthew', reported the *Observer*'s Kate Kellaway, 'is his Welshness.' By the same token the most striking aspect of the Rhys profiles is their fascination with the exotic details of a culture in which he was brought up a Methodist, spoke a language other than English both at home and school (a school, reported *The Times*, 'where rugby prowess was more prized than acting') and continued to rely on close links with family and school friends. The very attractive and yet nervous and self-conscious Rhys was obviously a youth from a different world, one, suggested Imogen Edwards-Jones, who 'hardly looks like a man who beds Turner for a living'. What could not be denied, however, was the demand for this young actor who in 2000 seemed to be in everything, including the film of *Titus Andronicus* in which his blond, tattooed and leather-clad Demetrius has his throat cut by Anthony Hopkins before being served up in a giant pie. The *Radio Times* found Rhys to be 'still the same mum-loving, Welsh rugby-loving lad he always was' and yet the casting directors could see that here was far more than a pretty face. This was a young man for our time, sensitive, anxious, alienated and given to mood swings between enthusiasm and apathy, with violence not being out of the question. His one major Welsh role had been in the film *House of America*, and his character Boyo, the middle son, though not always sure of where the action was heading had nevertheless conveyed beautifully the bruised experience of life in this dysfunctional family. The way in which a high colour suddenly floods into his pale face had become one of the most eloquent expressions of how youth in general had lost its bearings. Wales had given the English-speaking world one of the best exemplars of the X Generation.

Sara Sugarman's 2001 film *Very Annie Mary* was packed with detail and one of its minor pleasures was the scenes in which Matthew Rhys and Ioan Gruffudd played a gay couple who run the village café. Though largely undeveloped, the scenes constituted a lovely joke, for in the previous couple of years the London press had been bemused by the notion of friends who had been together at Melin Gruffudd Junior School, Ysgol Glantaf and RADA and who now shared a flat in Kilburn where they spoke only Welsh. 'The Boyos Done Good' was the headline of Garth Pearce's profile in the *Sunday Times*, one of many accounts of how these home-loving boys 'from the Valleys' innocently coped with the alien world of the big English-speaking city. It was out of such pieces that the notion of the Taff Pack developed.

If 2000 had been Matthew's year then it could be argued that 1999 and every year since had belonged to Ioan. Those of us who had missed him in *Pobol y Cwm* probably first saw Ioan when he struck what was a rare heroic note in *Titanic*. But it was his starring role in the four-part television series *Hornblower* that created a demand for his photograph and career details in every British and American newspaper. The name, of course, had to be explained; critics who had taken names such as Fiennes, Nighy, de la Tour, Malkovich and Mastrantonio in their stride found this unfamiliar Welsh agglomeration of vowels worthy of extensive analysis. 'As for the name', commented Jasper Gerard in the *Sunday Times*, 'they probably laugh about that in Merthyr Tydfil', almost as if he knew that Ioan had grown up in Aberdare. Gerard seemed preoccupied with the actor's long-time preference for Welsh girls, the long-delayed loss of his virginity, his Christianity and temporary connection with an evangelical cult, his homesickness for Wales and his affiliation to Plaid Cymru. Meanwhile, in the Welsh press there was rather less emphasis on the Freudian dimension and more on the actor's love of Welsh scenery, the Eisteddfod and the poetry of Alan Llwyd.

Certainly Ioan was reported on as an exotic, but all the while it had to be accepted that he was a 'hunk', a very handsome and authentically British heart-throb. His impact was best encapsulated in a January 2000 *Sunday Times* fashion article written by Alison Jane Reid and with photographs by Mike Owen. The piece was entitled 'An Officer and a Gentleman' and it was explained that 'classic, clean-cut lines always pass muster on fashion's front line – and it's a look that's perfectly suited to Ioan Gruffudd'. With his hair stylishly trimmed by 'Kerrie Williams at Joy Goodman' and, posing in a dark suit and a check suit, a maroon evening-wear sports jacket and a rib-knit polo-neck sweater (all chosen by the reporter), the actor looks every bit a professional model from an up-market magazine and, even more, as a genuinely important man around town. 'There is nothing quirky or trendy about him', argues the expert; 'he is classically good-looking', and as such 'is one of the first icons of the 21st century'. Owen's portraits are stunning and they certainly convey the sense of Gruffudd as a symbol of today's London, but the classic monochrome shot of the actor in the polo-neck carries all the powerful emotional appeal of a great Hollywood star of the era of *film noir*. We are dealing with seriously good looks.

Those looks and their undoubted appeal to female audiences have ensured his regular employment and his appearance in prestigious roles. Of course, the great danger for actors with classic good looks is that the screen will reveal that they have no hinterland, and in all those press profiles the subtext was the question of whether this boy from the Valleys was capable of generating real feeling and meaning in those parts that he was adorning. The answer to that query is that overall his performances have been mixed; clearly he needs to exercise care in his career choices. The role of Hornblower was his making and in many respects he was the ideal choice to play this great hero of the novel-reading middle classes. He was good in the action scenes, but his greatest quality as a television actor was the range of emotions he expressed in close-up. Gruffudd possesses one of the great noses of our time, its length seeming to vary from shot to shot, and with his equine nostrils, prominent cheekbones and large, dark, intense eyes he can rely on his head to do most of his acting. One senses his essential softness. The normally light voice suggests a degree of blandness which means that he can be upstaged by more definite and extrovert character acting. Nevertheless he can summon up indignation, and by slowing his delivery he can deepen his voice and convey real moral authority. The stilted nineteenth-century language allowed him to emphasize every syllable and express the genuine poetry in his voice.

*Hornblower* was first shown in the same year as *Warriors*, Leigh Jackson's two-part television drama depicting the role of British troops in the Bosnia of 1992. One wonders whether Gruffudd will ever be given better parts than these. As a young lieutenant having to deal with the complexities of policing ethnic rivalries, experiencing brutal atrocities and having to deal with his own and his men's psychological problems the Welsh actor was magnificent. Once again he was able to convey a natural authority; this young man was clearly a born leader. Always at his best in repose, he had a stillness that is almost unique in English-language television acting. The large brown eyes and expressive cheekbones convey the depth of feeling and the range of anxieties. One minute he is a handsome young man, the next a care-worn veteran contemplating suicide.

It is easy to see how Ioan Gruffudd's combination of essential goodness and facial expressiveness led to his casting in period drama. He was perfect as the adult Pip in the television *Great Expectations*, conveying gentility, humility, decency, anxiety, pleasure and, when he meets the grown-up Estella, real wonder. From the outset he was thoroughly Dickensian; in his stove hat he even looked a little like the young Dickens and one felt that here was an actor born to play David Copperfield. Alongside him, playing Herbert Pocket, was Daniel Evans continuously exuding authentic Dickensian enthusiasm and optimism. Gruffudd seemed slightly less at home in the movie *Wilde* where the emphasis was on his body rather than his face, but at least with his long hair he looked every inch the *fin de siècle* aesthete. He was far more at home in Paul Morrison's film *Solomon and Gaenor*, the Welsh-Jewish love story which was shot in Welsh/Yiddish and English/Yiddish versions and which earned an Oscar nomination. This retelling of the Romeo and Juliet story was rather undeveloped and underwritten but the early twentieth-century settings were perfect and it was beautifully photographed and sensitively played by Gruffudd and Nia Roberts in the title roles. I have often described Ioan's face as belonging to the Old Testament, and so convincing and moving was he in the part of a young Jewish lad that I was not surprised to read that he was eager to play Disraeli in a projected film about the Victorian statesman.

After these initial artistic successes Ioan Gruffudd has never ceased to be busy, but not all his selections have been wise and there are questions to be asked about his image and screen persona. The enormous popularity of *Hornblower* ensured a Hollywood debut but, for all his charm, *102 Dalmatians* did not suggest that light comedy is his forte. Following several forgettable and largely unnoticed British films he received massive advance publicity for the starring role in the television film of Tony Parsons's novel *Man and Boy*. In a very underwritten part he was mostly unconvincing and, facial expressions apart, seemed incapable of conveying inner passion. The main problem was a voice that, although effective in voice-overs, was too bland and unvaried to make any sense of the action scenes. He was quickly given a chance to redeem his reputation in ITV's remake of *The Forsyte Saga* in which he played the adulterer Bosinney. By the end of his contribution he had generated some real anger but, initially, he had once again seemed a bit bland, lacking in eroticism in the love scenes and somehow physically diminished, being shorter, slighter and more anonymous than one imagined him to be. Ioan Gruffudd has undoubtedly reached a turning point in his career. He is a very handsome and a very nice and honourable young man. Quite justifiably, however, international critics wonder whether he has a hinterland. To sustain his career he needs to inject a little devil into his acting and perhaps he should also lower his voice. He will not be able to play Pip all his life, and it is difficult to imagine this young Hornblower ageing into the wonderfully stoic character created by Gregory Peck. In all his interviews Ioan Gruffudd emphasizes that his greatest desire is to work in Wales on Welsh material, and yet when he did come home it was to play in the slight movie *Happy Now* in which his enigmatic police sergeant was upstaged by the photography of the Barmouth area. Surely the time has come for this actor to let rip with a performance in which he conveys something of his passion for Wales and for what Wales means in the contemporary world?

With both Matthew Rhys and Ioan Gruffudd one can sense that two very attractive Cardiff boys have stood out because of their looks, whilst all the time wondering whether their natural and satisfactory Welsh identities will be sufficient to sustain international careers. They both lack that natural love of thespian artifice and outrage that comes quite naturally, for example, to Daniel Evans. What is equally apparent is that the other two major stars who make up the Taff Pack are able to rely on raw talent as much as their looks, whilst their obvious professional intelligence leaves audiences in no doubt that they each have a hinterland. Rhys Ifans has appeared in a run of truly forgettable films, several of which did not even surface, but in two memorable roles and in countless interviews he gave a sure indication that he will be a major international film star. Meanwhile, in two stage roles Michael Sheen went straight to the top of the English theatre league table and even prompted Stephen Fry to assert that the actor would be going to the top of the list of great actors from Port Talbot. Apparently Burton and Hopkins were about to be eclipsed.

Ifans was born in Pembrokeshire but raised in Ruthin in north Wales. After Maes Garmon School in Mold and training at the Guildhall in London he served a theatrical apprenticeship at prestigious London venues. A growing frustration with audiences that he felt 'he didn't really know' led to his abandonment of the theatre and took him off to the contemporary music scene where he performed as lead singer with the Super Furry Animals. His great breakthrough came in Kevin Allen's 1997 film *Twin Town* in which he and his brother Llŷr starred as the central figures in a drug-inspired Swansea youth culture. A script with real wit and originality made this by far the most worthwhile and successful Welsh film of recent years. The occasional fallback onto stereotypes and clichés denied the film the international impact of the Scottish *Trainspotters*, but it none the less offered an effective satire of contemporary urban society, although there were some Swansea locals who thought the treatment of their town totally realistic. The tall leering Ifans was straight out of Dickens or any version of *The Threepenny Opera*, and one felt sure that most British cities possessed underworlds which were passing into the hands of such cynical rogues. For the role that was to take him to international stardom, that of Spike in the smash hit *Notting Hill*, Ifans did not have to make many adjustments. Armed with only a couple of T-shirts and a grubby pair of pants, he snatched the opportunity to turn in one of the most complete and effective examples of scene-stealing in the recent history of film. His impudent, zany and wonderfully self-confident Spike visibly took away the breath of stars Hugh Grant and Julia Roberts, and I loved reading the news that in the States distributors were having to add the name of Rhys Ifans to the posters advertising the film. A major movie fashioned as a slick comedy contrasting versions of English and American Cool had been stolen by a perfectly modulated display of Welsh chutzpah.

Ifans has explained his subsequent run of movie duck-eggs in terms of his wanting to escape from the Spike image. He made money and buttressed his Hollywood credentials in a number of supporting roles but, ironically, it might well be that it will be in playing upper-class and intellectual characters that he will find his true screen image. There was a hint of what was possible in his role as the visiting brother in the film of Brian Friel's *Dancing at Lughnasa*, and we suddenly became aware that his lean 6ft 3in. frame and innate intelligence gives him a truly patrician air. We had to wait several years for this to be confirmed. In *The Shipping News* his role as a somewhat eccentric English ex-public schoolboy who is trying to sail around the world was undeveloped but quietly promised much. 'It's nice to do a bit of posh', he told Rob Driscoll, and I suspect that there may be more of that to come. Interviews with and profiles of this charismatic and thoughtful actor are always worthwhile, and we can only hope that he encourages scriptwriters and directors in Los Angeles, London and Wales to exploit all his potential rather than going for the easy option.

In the 1950s Richard Burton had secured his reputation with two landmark performances: his playing of *Henry V* at Stratford in 1951 and then his entry into kitchen-sink cinema when he played Jimmy Porter in the film *Look Back in Anger* in 1959. He was too old and too patrician to be a truly effective Jimmy, but his selection for this iconic part in front of his theatrical rivals emphasized his standing in the profession. Almost half a century later, in the 1990s, the latest acting talent off the Port Talbot conveyor belt made the most of his opportunity in those very same parts. A prizewinner at RADA and much acclaimed for his theatre work in the mid-1990s, it was his 1997 Stratford Henry V which marked Michael Sheen out as one of the most powerful actors of the era. Ron Daniels's production in which 'First World War battlefield meets medieval French knights meets Hell's Angels' did not please everyone and neither did Sheen's king. The *Birmingham Post*'s Richard Edmonds found him 'boyishly likeable', but dressed as the president of a banana republic this king was too colloquial, lightweight, classless and without charisma. This critic seems to have missed the point, for what the majority of his colleagues appreciated was the way an apparent 'university student' was 'suddenly whisked to royal heights'. For the *Daily Express*'s Robert Gore-Langton 'a roisterer' had 'turned steely warrior', whilst for Charles Spencer, Sheen's king was 'a living oxymoron' who successfully brought everything together, for he could be 'warm and cold, determined and doubtful', cruel with the traitors and delightful when wooing Katherine. He thought 'the night belonged to Sheen', as did Linda Green of the *Coventry Evening Telegraph* who thought him 'superb as the passionate king urging his men into battle'. Nicholas De Jong in the *Evening Standard* thought Sheen 'the triumphant making of this production'.

It was obvious that the critics who saw *Henry V* at Stratford, the Barbican and on tour were struck by the fact that Sheen's appearance would not have automatically suggested royal stature. Paul Taylor of the *Independent* said that he was 'at once very virile and curiously elfin', whilst the *Financial Times*'s Alistair Macaulay referred both to his 'febrile quality' and to his 'rat-like brightness of eye and tooth'. Perhaps it was precisely the spelling out of these features that suggested that here was a natural Jimmy Porter. In 1999 Sheen was cast in this role in the National Theatre's revival of *Look Back in Anger*, the play which had made such an impact in 1956 that its significance has been debated by academics and theatre historians ever since. By 1999 the growing orthodoxy was that both the play and its impact had been greatly overrated and that Jimmy's anger did not really add up to much. From the outset it could be seen that Sheen was breathing new life into the part for, unlike Burton, he portrayed an authentic tenant of a seedy flat; his pop-eyed, round-shouldered and chesty Jimmy was giving vent to the frustration of a generation denied their place in the sun by an outdated establishment. The fact that this Jimmy was supported by an excellent cast, including Porthcawl's Jason Hughes as Welsh flatmate Cliff, helped to make this one of the theatrical events of the year. For the first time since Marlon Brando, an actor in a vest was the era's dramatic icon.

Sheen had come to the Osborne play from his continuing role as Mozart in the National's revival of Peter Shaffer's *Amadeus*. He was again a natural as the frenetic, overactive, immature genius, and not surprisingly it was the visit of this production to New York and Los Angeles that made Sheen a star in America where he has largely remained. Since 1995 he has lived with Kate Beckinsale, and with their daughter they have made their home in the States; obviously that is where their professional careers will be determined. The 2001 movie *Serendipity* confirmed that Kate is one of the most beautiful women in the world, and it is likely that this will help to give Hollywood every advantage in keeping yet another Port Talbot native away from the London stage. Those of us who saw him live in 1999 did well to take our opportunity.

What is frustrating about Sheen's absence is that no great Welsh actor has spoken so clearly about his artistic debt to Wales, and none has so decisively displayed his talent on Welsh soil. *Bright Smoke*, Paul Islwyn Thomas's 1998 television portrait of Sheen, is one of the best examinations and explanations of acting techniques I have ever seen; in it (and in many interviews too) the actor explained how much he owed to the West Glamorgan Youth Theatre and in particular to their courses at Dan-y-Coed, Swansea. His intensive training there is always in his mind and he often returns both in person and in his dreams. He explained how with every part he always starts by thinking 'can I do it Welsh?', and he outlined his continuing involvement with Welsh drama at that time, both as the founder of a theatre company to help young actors and as the director of *Badfinger*, Simon Harris's play set in a Swansea junk shop. The highlights of the film come in the form of two Shakespearean monologues which Sheen delivers to camera. We see him first walking on the mountain above Port Talbot, swigging beer and singing 'Ar Hyd y Nos'; suddenly he launches into the part of Romeo and we are in the midst of Shakespeare's great love story, only this time set in south Wales. The film ends with a scruffy lad sitting in a local park, and as he stands and walks towards us he becomes Henry V, urging us to action on St Crispin's Day, a speech that culminates very tellingly at Port Talbot's war monument. The cherubic Sheen looks so much like the young Dylan Thomas that one feels that he is destined to play the poet, but let us hope that someone responds to Paul Islwyn Thomas's lead by giving Welsh audiences some classically great acting either in Welsh drama or, as in those brief scenes of brilliance shot in and around Port Talbot, in standard works refined through the Welsh idiom.

The undoubted achievements of this group of actors, together with the massive publicity they received, were the basis of the Taff Pack conceit. At the twentieth century's end there was almost weekly confirmation that this was a golden era for Welsh popular culture. The Welsh rock groups were always in the news and, led by Michael Ball, there seemed to be a steady flow of Welsh talent into the vastly successful musicals that dominated the London stage. When the movie *American Psycho* was released in 2000 its star Christian Bale was identified in some reports as Welsh and it seemed for a while as if there was to be a new recruit to the Pack. 'Not since Hopkins's Lecter has a British actor been so brilliant at playing a baddie', said the *Sunday Times*, and I began to wonder what it was about Celtic good looks and charm that suggested the Welsh for these representations of pure evil. I confess that it was with some relief that I read a profile in which the indisputably saturnine and Pembrokeshire-born Bale described how he owed everything to his upbringing in Bournemouth.

Far more satisfying were all those theatre visits and reviews that confirmed that there was more to the flowering of Welsh acting than just three or four highly publicized stars. The Almeida's 1998 production of *The Iceman Cometh* starring Kevin Spacey was possibly London's highlight of the decade and contributing to the fine ensemble playing and American idiom were the Welsh actors Lisa Palfrey and Robert Pugh. In 2000 Phil Clark's production of Helen Griffin's *Flesh and Blood* played at the Hampstead Theatre and was acclaimed by metropolitan critics. Reading the programme it was deeply satisfying to reflect on the part played in the careers of the author and of the cast (Di Botcher, Brian Hibbard, Michelle McTernan and Stephen Meo) by Theatre West Glamorgan, the Sherman Theatre, the Welsh College of Music and Drama as well as *Cardiff East* and *Twin Town*. That evening in Swiss Cottage there was a sense that things were coming together very nicely in Welsh theatre. And all the while there were good London reviews for actors like Owen Teale, whom I had seen as a striking Hotspur at Stratford, and Mark Lewis Jones who had followed up *Cardiff East* with starring roles at the new Shakespeare's Globe

Theatre. At the millennium anyone following the British theatre scene could only conclude that if there was ever to be a time for a Welsh National Theatre this was it.

# Catherine Zeta Jones

Actors fulfil many functions within their cultures. They delineate, they complicate and they entertain. Occasionally there are individual stars whose role seems to consist very largely in allowing a culture to feel good about itself. By the late 1990s the dark-haired beauty Catherine Zeta Jones, who was born in Swansea in 1969, had achieved international fame and in Wales the frequent bulletins on her personal and professional life were read avidly. As she consolidated her position in the pecking order of Hollywood society and in that small elite group of women whose images sustain glossy international magazines, doing both with a surprising absence of angst or fuss, her Welsh fans basked in a degree of reflected glory. In what was a lacklustre era for the Welsh economy, it was the news of what was happening to Catherine Zeta (the industrialist Terry Mathews being her only rival in this respect) that confirmed that it was possible to escape from the goldfish bowl that was Wales and to prosper in a wider world. This particular actor had become our major export and virtually our only growth industry.

In the aftermath of the Second World War it was felt that my neighbourhood in Wales merited a community hall. I greatly enjoyed watching it being built and became a tea-boy for the workmen. Once it was open I became a regular patron, especially for those parties where we played games and then watched Chaplin and Popeye films. There were also talent competitions when family friends became crooners and when, invariably, we sat in total silence as a young girl from the council estate in her ballet costume danced to a piece of classical music. As ten-year-olds we were all in love with that ballerina and regarded her act as the year's cultural highlight. I had already become a film fan and fallen in love with the regular diet of Hollywood westerns and thrillers. I was rooted in a popular culture with two distinct streams, the local amateur bill of fare at the Alexandra Hall in Barry and the glossy world of Hollywood on offer at the three picture palaces just down the road. Quite simply, the story of Catherine Zeta Jones is that, three decades later, she was Swansea's equivalent of that young ballerina; but Catherine Zeta danced her way out of her local church hall right into the Hollywood that I had taken to exist only in the imagination.

When I returned to the cinema to see *The Vikings* and *Spartacus* for the second and third time (not least to relish Kirk Douglas's acting) I could not have anticipated the manner in which this great, indeed legendary, Hollywood actor would one day develop a Welsh connection. More than anybody else in recent history, Catherine Zeta has walked out of an everyday Wales and into a mythology. For centuries in the Middle Ages the Welsh waited for a prince who would be a *mab darogan*, a 'son of destiny'. Such is the hype that there are times when I begin to wonder whether young Dylan, the son of Swansea's Catherine Zeta Jones and Hollywood's Michael Douglas (son of Kirk), is not the prince for which the Wales of today is waiting.

In 2002 it was announced that Catherine Zeta Jones had signed a £5 million deal with the giant cosmetics company Elizabeth Arden and that she would be appearing in an international photo campaign advertising the latest fragrance under the caption 'What is beauty?'. A company spokesman explained that she would be joining Liz Hurley, Andie MacDowell and Isabella Rossellini as Arden supermodels and that she had been chosen because of her 'classic looks' and because 'she is the epitome of personal style, elegance and sophistication'. We were hardly surprised by this news as Catherine Zeta had been featured in most of the recent lists of the world's most beautiful women. In 2000, when the American magazine *Company* listed her as the only British woman in 'The 50 Most Beautiful People in The World' (and only two British men made the cut: Jude Law and Rupert Everett), *Wales on Sunday*'s Suzie Brewer immediately responded by putting Catherine top of her list of 'The 50 Most Beautiful People in Wales'. I was in the process of concurring with Suzie's list in which Catherine came in first, immediately ahead of Lisa Rogers and Jan Anderson, when I realized that this was meant to be an all-time adjudication. The fact that Owain Glyndŵr was at number 27 and Lloyd George at number 47 in the list indicates not only that Miss Brewer was struggling but also the extent to which millennial Wales was in awe of its favourite new star. I was more interested in *Hello*'s 2002 list of 'Britain's 25 Most Beautiful Women' headed by Kate Beckinsale. My initial reaction was one of disappointment, for the Swansea star came in only twenty-first, one place behind Elizabeth Hurley. But the competition was strong, with Yasmin Le Bon, Julie Christie, Jemima Khan and Nigella Lawson thoroughly deserving their high ratings. This was good popular journalism, for the readers who had been polled and the judges (including Angharad Rees) had clearly taken into consideration things other than the purely superficial. This exercise deserved careful thought. I was delighted to see Catherine justly take her place in this exalted company and concluded that, if justice had been done, she should have been in eleventh or twelfth position.

That such beauty should come out of Swansea is no surprise to those of us who have served time in the dance halls of Mumbles and the night-clubs of the Kingsway. There is, of course, a whole literature attesting to the power of attractive Swansea girls to disorientate vulnerable males. In his fictional memoir of the town, *Portrait of the Artist as a Young Dog*, Dylan Thomas recalled the girl spotted in Victoria Gardens who had a 'Woolworth's white rose' in her chestnut hair. She was a 'girl in a million' who 'took his long look to herself, and cherished his stupid love'; she was 'a piece of God help us all right'. When Kingsley Amis lived in Swansea, his all too apparent interest in young women was rewarded by his being asked to judge a local beauty competition. The experience resulted in a poem in which Dai Evans, during the judging of 'Miss Glamorgan (West) 1963' sees in Miss Clydach's 'hip-swing, rich bosom and mean face – his own destruction'. Even more memorable and pertinent was the opening of Amis's novel *That Uncertain Feeling* in which we read of the reaction of John Lewis when local socialite Mrs Elizabeth Gruffydd-Williams walks into Aberdarcy library. Casting directors considering yet another film version of this novel should note that Mrs Gruffydd-Williams is described as being 'a woman of thirty or thirty-five', with 'wide dark eyes, dark, rather thick eyebrows, skin the colour of the top of the milk and hair the colour of tar'. Having studied the lady well, what excited the librarian Lewis most was his conclusion that 'some things about her appearance and mannerisms seemed to indicate that a certain basic human activity never entered her thoughts, others that it never left them'. How often has that precise point been made in descriptions of Catherine Zeta's qualities?

As she established herself as a major international star and at the same time entered her thirties it became fashionable to talk of the way in which she was 'a real woman' and, as such, a throwback to the classic Hollywood years of the 1950s. There was almost a sense of relief in some quarters that the age of blonde teeny-boppers was giving way to one in which stories would revolve around dark, mature *femmes fatales*. In January 2001 *Vanity Fair* chose to highlight her 'combination of sex and toughness', qualities that put 'her in a class with the stars of Hollywood's golden age', and which were to be brilliantly encapsulated in accompanying photographs by Mario Testino. It struck Jon Amiel, who directed her in *Entrapment*, that Catherine 'is one of the first actresses since the days of Elizabeth Taylor and Lana Turner and Ava Gardner to bring that full-blown, luscious, ripe-rose sexuality to the screen'. For Jan de Bont, who directed her in *The Haunting*, 'there's a kind of danger to a woman like Catherine: she is definitely not an innocent, she's not really her age; she's had too much life experience'.

Catherine Zeta's sexual danger and hour-glass figure were most memorably captured in Mario Testino's most widely used studies of her in a one-piece strapless laced black bodice. Here we see how, in Amiel's phrase, she was capable of oozing a 'honeyed sexuality'. And yet the director went on to comment on her 'incredible wholesomeness and naturalism'. Many others have noted that her sex appeal came as part of a general exuberance and unaccompanied by any affectation or design. This undoubtedly raises the question of whether she is as lacking in innocence as de Bont suggests. The photographer Patti Boyd has spoken of her as 'a classic Welsh beauty' and one with 'an innocence within her beauty'. Whether it is entirely innocent or not, there is certainly a child-like element in her face which belies the straightforward comparisons with Ava Gardner and the other stars of the era of *film noir*. Catherine herself has spoken of her 'piggy nose' and 'puffy eyes'. Looked at in close-up those eyes ('hazel' or 'almond'?) have an undoubted oriental cast and, furthermore, are the eyes of a very young oriental. Is there yet a child's softness and incompleteness to the face that will prevent her from being as powerful an exponent of mature female sophistication as were the truly magnificent Gardner and Taylor?

Many things have changed since Hollywood's classic years, but what is remarkable is that, for all the new feminism, we still have difficulty in coming to terms with the connection between female glamour and the acting profession. There is hardly a major female star today who has not had difficulty in finding worthwhile and challenging parts. Both movie producers and audiences alike take female sexual attractiveness for granted and consistently underrate the acting skills of the leading stars. In these respects responses to Catherine provide a classic example of all the sloppy thinking that surrounds stardom. In a revealing profile in which he attempted to analyse what it is about her 'that tinges admiration with suspicion', Ed Potton referred to the star's 'God-given curves'. All too easily the critics and their readers have assumed that it was only what was God-given that accounted for her success – hence the necessity in interview after interview for the star to emphasize both the extent of her formal training and the sheer determination and character needed to sustain the career. Perhaps it will only be with the release of *Chicago* that the world will realize that Catherine Zeta Jones is a trained dancer who, between the ages of four and fifteen (when she moved full-time to London), had received the best dance and singing training that Swansea, a town chock-full of amateur drama and musical companies, could offer. She has always been both attractive and accomplished.

The beauty of the great cliché at the core of the musical *42nd Street* is that it encapsulates exactly the mythology of show business in which audiences want to believe. But, of course, the actress playing Peggy Sawyer, the ingénue who steps in to take over from the indisposed star, has to have the necessary talent and technique. All the world knows that after earlier roles in *Annie* and *Bugsy Malone* it was Catherine's real-life elevation from second understudy to star in the triumphant *42nd Street* at London's Drury Lane that put her on the road to success. The next significant stepping stone was the twelve-episode television comedy-drama series *The Darling Buds of May* which began in 1991. The series picked up a cult following and, to an extent that they could never have anticipated, the stars became household names. It was her persona as the voluptuous pubescent Mariette Larkin that rocketed Catherine into the tabloids and made both her professional and personal details subjects of constant speculation. It was at this stage that she must have come to understand what strength of character was required to protect her identity and integrity in the mad world in which the press assumed that stars, and especially starlets, belonged to them. For the two years of the *Darling Buds* craze she was hounded by the paparazzi and it was this that encouraged the move to Hollywood. The lessons were clear; all the while a successful actress has to nurture and extend her talents and skills, has to remain fit and stylish, has to exercise care in the choice of roles and has to manage and control relationships with producers and the press. The challenges are immense, and one always knows that the slightest fall from grace will be front-page news, that to appear topless, even at a private pool, will gift some anonymous photographer half a million pounds. Catherine Zeta Jones has come through all of this triumphantly, but it took more than 'God-given curves' and 'honeyed sexuality'. What it took was ambition and discipline. In 2000, when success was assured, she summed it all up by commenting: 'I got here on my own bloody hard work and perseverance.'

The nature of Catherine Zeta's achievement was subjected to intense scrutiny at the time of her wedding to Michael Douglas in New York in November 2000. The occasion was the very stuff of what today passes as hot news, and across the world journalists vied with each other as they milked the event for every detail, and especially every incongruity. This was the day when 'the red dragon of Wales fluttered over New York's Plaza Hotel', when Welsh lamb, Caerphilly cheese and Brain's beer were on the menu, when stars like Jack Nicholson 'danced the night away' with the bride's elderly relatives and when the rings exchanged were valued at £7,000 and were made of Welsh gold. Of course, in all the reporting, there was an element of disapproval. The bride might look like 'Snow White' in her £100,000 diamond-encrusted cream David Emanuel dress but this particular fairy-tale had been far too cleverly negotiated for the popular press. They could not forget that the £1m picture deal with *OK!* magazine had excluded all other reporters and that a prenuptial agreement negotiated by the bride's brothers, David and Lyndon, had given her every financial protection in the event of a divorce or of the husband having 'a fling'. However, what had really rankled was the information that guests had been asked not to give presents but to donate to a trust fund for the couple's three-month-old son.

Almost certainly it was the coolness with which the details of this truly dynastic marriage had been negotiated that took away the breath of journalists and forced them to play up the folkloric and mythical dimensions of the occasion. All the television and photographic evidence suggested that the two families, the Joneses of Swansea and the Douglases of California, went to the Plaza Hotel as social equals; if anybody looked like film stars it was Catherine's parents, Dai and Pat.

What certain sections of the press clearly wanted was a scenario in which Welsh hillbillies rubbed shoulders with the American film aristocracy. The line taken was in keeping with the general tendency to treat her as a girl from the sticks whose 'curves' had given her fame and fortune which she was now consolidating by marrying a wealthy superstar twenty-five years her senior. This 'daughter of working-class Wales' from 'the tiny Welsh fishing village of Mumbles' had 'tap-danced her way through a small-town childhood' and consequently had been able to take herself 'from Swansea's backstreets to the dizzy heights of Tinseltown's royalty'. She had to be 'the Valleys girl'; nobody wanted to read about a suburban middle-class girl who had staked out a successful professional career and who was now coolly accepting the logic of the status to which her skills had entitled her.

Our modern tabloid press is characterized by a fundamental paradox in its attitude to those very celebrities who constitute its basic raw material. It wants us, its readers, to be fascinated by the details of individual success and yet to be mildly resentful of it. The basic challenge facing stars like Catherine Zeta Jones is that of not giving the press the satisfaction of things going wrong. Yet, in her case she has won through to an even greater victory. The orthodoxy was that after considerable success in *The Darling Buds of May*, in which it was thought that she had been typecast, she had failed to develop as an actress and been forced to appear in mediocre movies in which her looks were everything. To see her now in the dreadful 1993 movie *Splitting Heirs* is to realize all the shortcomings of the British film industry at that time. The script was third-rate, but what was shameful was that in 1993 nobody seemed to see that in the part of the sexy gold-digger determined to marry the duke and move into his castle there was a very good comic actress. Her performance was delightful, unaffected and convincing, and she was the best thing in the movie. But she had to go to Hollywood and be 'spotted' by Steven Spielberg in the television mini-series *Titanic* before anyone realized that she was a genuine actress. Then there followed *The Mask of Zorro, Entrapment, High Fidelity, Traffic* and *America's Sweethearts*. Having seen the latter, the critic Ed Potton found himself wondering whether she 'has actually become a decent actress'. Of course, any decent critic would have spotted this several years earlier. Catherine Zeta's greatest triumph over the press (and, one suspects, many of its readers, perhaps not least in Wales) turned out to be quite simply that she is good.

I have a feeling that Spielberg's *The Mask of Zorro* will be remembered as the film that most effectively deployed her unique combination of talents. This romp was planned as the next step in the irresistible rise of heart-throb Antonio Banderas, but his co-star more than held her own and actually captured most of the headlines, not least as she came across as the most authentically Mexican element in the film. Hollywood had always known about the beauty of the 'black Irish', but here the Swansea girl, well aware of her Irish blood, was releasing all the considerable *hauteur* and style of what she herself describes as the 'black Welsh'. She looked as if all her life she had been duelling on her hacienda with a rose between her teeth. It was her dancing and movement skills which also carried her through *Entrapment*. This was more good fun but less convincing than *Zorro*, for the whole thing seemed like a training exercise, almost as if Sean Connery were really testing this young lady. That she came through with flying colours was confirmation of her physical fitness and sheer professionalism. I was delighted to read subsequently that she had learned a great deal off-screen from the veteran Scot about how to retain one's dignity in the mad world of southern California.

Her breakthrough dramatic role came in *Traffic*. It was undoubtedly a brave decision for the six-months-pregnant actor to accept the role of the debt-ridden wife of an imprisoned drug baron, but she rose to the challenge superbly. It was good to see her 'out of costume' and playing someone rather like herself. Surely, after *Chicago* this is the direction her career must follow. She was relaxed in the early scenes and then generated all the anguish and anger needed to sustain her big dramatic moments. Swansea audiences were amused to hear a familiar Treboeth cadence when she described something as being 'terrific', but what has been referred to as her 'Welsh-British-American twang' sounded exactly right for the European Beverley Hills socialite that she was playing. She was also perfectly cast as the wealthy party girl in *High Fidelity*, and she swaggered her way through that cameo with all the arrogance and confidence of someone who knew that Hollywood was hers. Strangely, her best reviews came for *America's Sweethearts*, not least because many critics felt that in the role of a spoilt and temperamental actress she was playing herself. In the *Irish Times* Michael Dwyer rightly highlighted the 'butchy relish' of Catherine's playing, but one was aware that too often she was having to overdo things to disguise the thinness of the script. In *Zorro* she had delivered a 'sizzling' sexuality: here the kinky sex scene seemed tired. Quietly, in the role of the ugly duckling sister, Julia Roberts turned in a performance that was more nuanced and stole the film. I hope that on this occasion further professional lessons were learnt by Catherine Zeta and her management team.

With *Chicago* about to be released and a romantic comedy starring George Clooney, Hollywood's man of the moment, in the pipeline, Catherine Zeta Jones stands at the peak of her profession. Guided by her astute brothers, Hollywood producers in their own right, and drawing on the ability of her husband to recognize good material, she is guaranteed a period of successful and rewarding work. Her great triumph is richly deserved. She was a talented child performer who was determined to maximize her opportunities, and the adoption of her grandmother's name in an attempt to mark herself out from all the other Catherine Joneses was just the stylish and exotic touch necessary to send her on her way. Many still photographs emphasize the true extent of her striking good looks, and now an increasing number of movies indicate how interesting she is as a person. Directors will always be tempted to tease out the exotic and predatory in her, but I hope we see more of her in the *Traffic* mode, for surely the point about Catherine Zeta now is how remarkable she is in her own right. We should be allowed to see on screen exactly those inner qualities that took her from Treboeth to Beverley Hills. In America, the star system is one that gives the country an aristocracy. Kirk Douglas and his son Michael won their places in that elite. Now they have been joined by the young lady described by *The Times* as 'the Princess from Wales'. Yes, she is our princess. But we are all allowed our private fantasies: for me, Catherine Zeta is essentially Swansea's Mrs Gruffydd-Williams who dresses up in a Mexican costume for her fencing lessons.

# *A* *Nation of Actors*

A nation's culture emerges out of a network of debates and preoccupations. To come to terms fully with contemporary Wales we would certainly have to devote a significant amount of time to studying the state of its theatre. It could be argued that the prolonged and sometimes bitter debate on the whole question of contemporary drama in Wales has been more vital and riveting than that on any other public issue. Yet it can hardly be claimed that the protagonists in this soul-searching exchange of views have captured the nation's attention. Essentially, the whole matter has constituted a subculture. The importance of contemporary drama has not been confronted squarely, and in relegating this vibrant strand in its national life Wales has undoubtedly missed a crucial opportunity to establish a mature identity in terms of both domestic and international perception.

Contemporary Welsh theatre has been sustained by a small number of dramatists who, in general, have been far less well known than their colleagues who write poetry or prose. Quite crucially, after indigenous theatre companies have staged these dramatists, a small band of critics and academics have analysed and debated both texts and performances. The drama scene begins with writers like Greg Cullen, Dic Edwards, Ed Thomas, Charlie Way and Frank Vickery before passing into the hands of companies such as the Sherman, Y Cwmni, Moving Being, Volcano and Hijinx as well as various youth enterprises. The small audiences are the direct beneficiaries of the various productions but, mercifully, critics such as David Adams, Gilly Adams, Jeni Williams and Hazel Walford Davies are usually present. Their achievement has been the writing of this drama into our national culture, initially in the press and journals and then in a more formal academic context. And all the while they are joined by directors such as Phil Clark and Michael Bogdanov and countless administrators and politicians who want far more money to be invested in Welsh drama and who think that its Cinderella status will only end when the nation confronts the issue of whether it should have a national theatre.

In the debate on Welsh drama there has been a growing and very natural emphasis on texts and on the fact that this is a writers' medium.

However, critics have never failed to be excited by the performances themselves, and undoubtedly it is the degree to which that excitement has been communicated which forms the cutting edge of the debate. Hazel Walford Davies and David Adams very quickly picked up on Ceri Sherlock's description of Welsh culture as being essentially 'performative'. Most thrilling in recent years have been revolutionary and challenging stagings by Y Cwmni and Volcano and breathtakingly innovative productions by directors such as Firenza Guidi. Very noticeably, amidst all this excitement comparatively little attention is given to the question of acting, and yet to the cultural historian one of the most interesting aspects of the whole phenomenon is the effortless way in which theatre companies, whether independent or school or college based, are able to draw on a seemingly never-ending supply of young actors. As a nation we publicly mourned the passing of our coal miners and our steel workers and yet we failed to appreciate the silent revolution that made us a nation of actors. As crucial as anything in our culture was the way in which educationalists in the last decades of the twentieth century sensed that there were untapped riches in our schools and that it was time to move beyond the routine study of set texts for public examinations. The youth of Wales were invited to take to the boards and, so, all over the country young individuals found new confidence and, in increasing numbers, new careers as they acted at first with their fellow students and then for professional companies or television.

As a culture we cherish public recognition and celebrity more than actual achievement and so it is that we hear little about the individual triumphs in actual productions of the National Youth Theatre of Wales and rather more about the way particular students from Ysgol Glanaethwy, Gorseinon College or Rhydfelen have won places at RADA. 'Three Aim for Stage Stardom' was the *South Wales Evening Post*'s headline as they reported that 'three budding thespians from Gorseinon College have landed places at the prestigious Royal Academy for the Dramatic Arts'. It was further explained that only one in every hundred applicants succeeds, and naturally there was delight that Alex Beckett, Bethan Evans and Kwaku Ankomah were all embarking on the three-year professional acting diploma. A year later came the news that Rhiannon James, a former student of Olchfa School and Swansea College and a member of the National Youth Theatre of Wales and West

Glamorgan County Youth Theatre, having finished her degree at Birmingham, had won a place at RADA. According to the *Evening Post* she was 'one of 1,600 applicants' and 'after three tough auditions, she was one of only 34 hopefuls chosen'. The report ended with the sobering note that Rhiannon was now 'looking for sponsorship from the business community to help fund her financial commitments at RADA'.

Overwhelmingly, the public perception of the acting profession is formed by television and, accordingly, when next we read about aspiring youngsters it is when they have landed parts in televised drama. In 2001 *Evening Post* readers learned that nineteen-year-old Lisa Zahra of Morriston, who had studied at Gorseinon College before going on to the Welsh College of Music and Drama, had joined the cast of the HTV drama series *Nuts and Bolts*, playing the part of 'a rather snooty student' called Abigail. 'I have always wanted to act since I was tiny', explained Lisa, 'and I've done a lot of stage work with West Glamorgan Youth Theatre and Swansea Amateur Operatic Society.' In the series she was acting alongside nineteen-year-old Mathew Evans who had been a fellow student at Gorseinon, whilst one of the leading writers of the stories was another Gorseinon and West Glamorgan Youth product Neil Anthony. A fascinating insight into the extent to which television soaps like *Nuts and Bolts* now shape the educational process was provided by the *Western Mail* story that a group of students at Trinity College, Carmarthen had, as part of their course, produced a magazine series called *Lysh* for broadcast on S4C Digital. Out of that project the students (under the direction of Eurof Williams and with the help of former *Crossroads* writer Hazel Wyn Williams) developed their own hall of residence-based soap called *Slysh*, which would form a strand within the magazine format. Siân Thomas, who had been a member of the team, explained that the aim had been 'to provide entertainment with plenty of emotion, humour and sensationalism without being afraid to push the boundaries about life as a college student'. One is bound to feel that at such moments we are catching glimpses of a new Wales which will be dominated by moguls every bit as influential as the Warner brothers or Samuel Goldwyn.

Television in Wales, however, can only represent a start. Everybody knows which programmes it is that are watched by devoted and mass audiences, and what the local press should celebrate is the appearance of our young actors in the soaps which dominate British television viewing, not least because over the years there has been a widespread perception that Wales has been underrepresented in this vitally important regard. Adrian Lewis Morgan from Beddau trained at the Welsh College of Music and Drama and then secured parts in West End musicals such as *Sweeney Todd* at the National, but all the while (explained the *Western Mail*) 'half of him secretly hankered for a different kind of fame – from television'. Then came the story that he was receiving national publicity for his role in BBC1's *Holby City*. In his part of Liam he was about to be accused of raping another nurse who, incidentally, was being played by the Welsh actress Anna Mountford. Clearly Adrian was enjoying his national publicity, but he made it plain that as the son of musical parents he felt that it was in that direction that his career would develop. A few months later the *Evening Post* was celebrating the fact that 'a Gwendraeth Valley hunk' called Matt Zarb, who was born in north Wales but educated in Kidwelly, was 'setting the screen alight as Toyah's new love interest in *Coronation Street*'. He is cast as a Croatian, but Matt pointed out that he had 'a nan in Pontyates' and that he missed the people in Wales – 'they're much friendlier'. One success story that afforded the Welsh media particular pleasure was that of Jan Anderson. Jan, who was born in Brecon and raised in Porthcawl, had received an enormous amount of publicity in 1997 when, at the age of twenty-two, she played the part of sixteen-year-old Jody in the BBC Wales series *Tiger Bay*, the soap that was intended to mark the arrival of Cardiff's Drama Department as a significant provider of network drama. In the event the series did not survive its opening run and the cast had to look elsewhere. The stunningly attractive Jan was much in demand as a cover girl and model but she found regular employment playing the lively staff nurse Chloe Hill in the BBC's *Casualty*. As a BBC soap star, fulfilment for Jan had come in studios in Bristol and not Cardiff, the city she regarded as her home base.

Wales was clearly enjoying the new-found and potential celebrity of its young stars, but occasionally there were warning signs that fame and fortune could not be taken for granted. Nia Roberts, who had gone from Brecon High School and the National Youth Theatre of Wales to Birmingham University, made her professional debut in S4C's *Halen yn y Gwaed* before achieving fame and acclaim for her highly sensitive acting in the Oscar-nominated film *Solomon a Gaenor* and in Eurwyn Williams's delicate treatment of undergraduate anxiety *Lois*. In 2001, however, it was reported that Nia was finding it difficult to secure work in Wales and was currently looking more to London and Hollywood. She told the *Western Mail*'s Karen Price that familiarity was the problem, adding that 'in Wales, the more you do, the less they want to use you'. At much the same time Price was hearing similar complaints from Maria Pride, the Rhydfelen and Aberystwyth-trained actress who, having been acclaimed for her roles in the BBC dramas *Care* and *Score*, found herself unemployed for several months. Both Nia and Maria made unfavourable comparisons between conditions prevailing in Wales and England. They felt that in the latter one was not 'penalised for doing good work'; on the contrary, argued Maria, programmes would be created for promising young actors. Meanwhile the *Evening Post* reported that Robert Statham, the Swansea-based actor who had appeared in *Casualty* and was now performing with the Fluellen Theatre Company whilst working as a job trainer with the Welsh Initiative for Supported Employment, was desperately seeking assistance to help him pay £7,500 for a course at a London theatre college. The question that clearly arises is whether we have fully worked out the consequences of having created a sizeable pool of acting talent.

What is beyond dispute is that drama and the profession of acting have secured a significant and prominent place in contemporary Welsh life. On its own this fact should not really surprise cultural historians for, although receiving surprisingly little attention, amateur dramatics have been a vibrant feature of village and urban life in Wales since the 1930s. Subsequently (and again as a result of initiatives largely ignored by commentators) television executives, educationalists and community workers built on these foundations to ensure that there would be at least one expanding profession in post-industrial Wales. It was only the extensive British and international publicity attending the identification of the Taff Pack which finally alerted people to what they took to be the new phenomenon of Welsh drama. In fact, a far more significant development than the attention given to a small number of stars was that Welsh actors had established an impressive degree of professional competence across the whole spectrum of film and television, both in Wales and the wider world. The great achievement of S4C, BBC Wales and HTV has been to commission drama that has allowed a generation of Welsh actors to depict convincingly and entertainingly the realities of the nation's everyday life. To a degree the stereotypes persist, for we appear to cherish traditional modes of discourse and especially humour. Another failing has been that of slavishly accepting English models by assuming that everything that succeeds there has to be replicated. There have been many false dawns and changes of direction as BBC Wales, in particular, has searched for the appropriate formula and level for developing drama that would appeal outside Wales. But amidst the hype and confessions we have undoubtedly moved on, and in series like *Tair Chwaer*, *Nuts and Bolts* and *Belonging* there have been moments, often accompanied by tears of laughter or sorrow, when we have been given an understanding of the real passions that characterize our society. Here drama allows us to get behind the tabloid headlines, pointing as it does to real emotional complexities.

Within Wales actors such as Donna Edwards, Richard Harrington, Eve Myles and Stephen Meo have been broadening our sense of our own community whilst slowly but surely Welsh actors have been establishing a presence in British television drama generally. In 1999 Mark Lewis Jones explained what a breakthrough it had been that in the ITV drama series *The Knock* he had been cast as a customs officer, a part he had been allowed to play as a Welsh character though it had not been written as such. At auditions he now invariably used his own accent. 'Thank God', he exclaimed, 'gone are the days when you had to justify being Welsh.' Of course, personality is of the essence in acting, as Mark had realized, and it was undoubtedly this enhanced understanding that prepared him for the leading role he was to play in BBC Wales's successful series *The Bench*. After decades of neglect Welsh characters began to appear in British soaps and drama series. Before returning to Wales for *Nuts and Bolts*, Ammanford's Richard Ellis had played the hippy Huw Edwards in *EastEnders*, just as Neath's Robert Gwilym, remembered for his role alongside his brother Mike in the film *On the Black Hill*, had an effective run in *Casualty*. The comparatively new interdependence of English and Welsh television drama is perhaps best illustrated in the career of Charles Dale, the Tenby-born actor who appeared with the Tenby Players, the Torch Youth Theatre in Milford Haven and the National Youth Theatre before training in London. Dale came to prominence playing a womanizer in the popular BBC series *The Lakes* before moving on to *Coronation Street* and the role of the biker Dennis. By the time the character of Dennis was killed in a car crash Dale had already established himself as the mechanic Steve in *Belonging*. This was his first Welsh role and it came after twenty years in which nobody had realized his nationality. In 2002 he starred in *Paradise Heights*, a BBC1 family saga. 'I suppose my accent's gone', he told Rob Driscoll, 'but my Welshness hasn't', adding that 'it gives you a little bit of soul; I think Welsh actors are more lyrical – in touch with their feelings'.

As the Welsh establish their rightful position in the British repertory company perhaps two actors stand out. In 2001 Robert Pugh played a soccer manager in BBC Wales's *Score* and, at the same time, he was starring in BBC2's *In a Land of Plenty* as a domineering industrialist. Already, in the television remake of Evelyn Waugh's *Sword of Honour* and the film *Enigma*, he had shown that he had cornered the market in irate military types. Meanwhile Rob Brydon from Porthcawl, who after training in Cardiff had worked as an actor and presenter on television and for BBC Radio Wales, followed his enormously successful series of BBC2 monologues *Marion and Geoff* by playing the same character in a one-off play, *A Small Summer Party*. All the evidence suggested that Brydon's highly original creation, the cuckolded cab driver Keith Barrat, would be returning to national television in one format or another. Here was a timely reminder to Welsh television planners that experiment, freshness, originality and ambition should be the basis of drama aimed at British audiences.

At the start of the new century it was with considerable pleasure that one noted the success of Welsh actors in every medium. From the Birmingham Rep came news of Rakie Ayola's triumphs as Viola in *Twelfth Night* and Ophelia in *Hamlet*. In *The Times* Jeremy Kingston praised her 'bright-eyed wondering' innocence as Viola, whilst in a televised clip of her Ophelia what struck me was her flawless enunciation in which every word was made to count and every phrase was given full emotional and intellectual value. Meanwhile, the Welsh were claiming positions in the military platoons so loved by international film producers. In Ridley Scott's timely study of American counter-terrorist tactics, *Black Hawk Down*, one American soldier was played by former RADA student Ian Virgo who was born in Caldicot. The big television series of 2001 was Steven Spielberg's *Band of Brothers*, the story of the 101st Airborne Division's role in the liberation of Europe, and in this hugely expensive production another former RADA student, Nicholas Aaron from Pontardawe, played the role of 'Popeye' Wynn.

As always, successful theatrical productions triggered off further speculation about the need for a national theatre in Wales. The *Lear* that Theatr Clwyd brought to Cardiff in 2001 was the clearest and most coherent I have ever seen. In Terry Hands's production, Nicol Williamson convincingly embodied nearly all of the king's kaleidoscope of moods whilst, in this ensemble play, a company of mostly young Welsh actors memorably filled out the action. Jenny Livsey (Regan), Siwan Morris (Cordelia), Julian Lewis-Jones (Kent), Steffan Rhodri (Gloucester) and Ifan Huw Dafydd (Cornwall) were especially effective. In the summer of 2002 Michael Bogdanov ingeniously staged *The Merry Wives of Windsor* beneath the walls of Ludlow Castle. Philip Madoc was Falstaff, but in an acclaimed production of what is also an ensemble piece it was the playing of the largely Welsh company which caught the eye. David Adams pointed out that 'the cream of Welsh theatre was on show' and highlighted the playing of Russell Gomer, Simon Armstrong, Eve Myles, Darren Thomas and newcomer Morgan Rhys. For Adams, this was 'easily one of the best Welsh Shakespeare productions' he had ever seen but, of course, he was left wondering why he had to cross into England to see it.

And yet, as we savour the degree to which the Welsh investment in acting has paid off, we are still left with the feeling that anticipation runs ahead of achievement. There are still far too few good feature films, and no Welsh film has yet broken through internationally, either in box-office or critical terms. All the while we wait for Welsh television drama to make it to the British networks, at the same time bemoaning the lack of first-class professional theatre in our capital city. It seems that we train actors in schools, youth and community projects more as a sociological exercise than as a cultural investment. Surely it is not the case that our young people become actors because there is nothing else to do or because we still remain hostile to careers in business and technology. Hopefully, acting is not our last resort. Perhaps we are content that our indigenous theatre remains an underground subcultural phenomenon. But surely the time is now ripe for our writers, producers and arts providers to become more ambitious and to claim their space at the forefront of our culture. It would be iniquitous if we were to allow the careers of Matthew Rhys, Paul Rhys, Rakie Ayola and their colleagues to develop any further without their being given the chance to act out the significance of their Welshness. It is appalling that the great theatre work of Jonathan Pryce, Daniel Evans, Michael Sheen and Des Barrit is not seen in Cardiff, Swansea and the rest of Wales. In 2001 Kate Burton, Richard's daughter, was the toast of Broadway after her stunning performances in *Hedda Gabler*. If we had any claims to be a nation dedicated to the theatre, that production should have been brought to Cardiff. As we read that Patrick Jones's play *Everything Must Go* excited critics at the Lyric Hammersmith, that Gary Owen's *The Shadow of a Boy* was one of the earliest productions at the National Theatre's new loft, and that Sheffield's Crucible Theatre staged Peter Gill's *Cardiff Plays*, we gain some insight into what it would be like if Cardiff were a city dedicated to placing theatre at the centre of Welsh life. Anthony Hopkins, Catherine Zeta-Jones, John Rhys-Davies and the rest of the Welsh colony in Hollywood should be made to feel that it is yet Wales that will give them artistic fulfilment. There is no reason why we should not aim to create a permanent theatrical and cinematic buzz both in our capital city and the rest of Wales.

When Richard Burton confessed that, if born a couple of decades earlier, he would have been in the pulpit and not on the stage, he was doing far more than making the obvious point that the Welsh like to perform in public whatever the platform. Rather, he was implying that whatever the nature of performances they reflect the culture in which they were fashioned. As I have already argued, the essence of Burton's greatness was that within his acting was the potential for him to be our spiritual leader, our prime minister or our greatest novelist. He had wanted to be those things, and those desires informed his acting. Subsequently, all those actors who have claimed that there is a special dimension to Welsh acting are recognizing the extent to which they are products of a specific set of cultural circumstances. It is the job of those actors, working in conjunction with writers, to tease out all those elements of their times which have contributed to their unique artistic identity. Just as Burton was the product of a distinctive bilingual urban culture, so the new generation of Welsh actors is one that has been thrown up by a society which has undergone dramatic social change. There is drama enough in the collapse of industry, in the virtual disappearance of Christian faith and in the discovery of new energies, both in an old language and in a new music. In contemporary Wales there have been shocks and surprises aplenty, and it is a thing of great wonder that we have young people eager to express their sense of frustration and relief artistically. We have shown that we can direct our musical talents into new modes, and there is plenty of evidence that we can publicly articulate a whole range of complex emotions. Every month now there is evidence of increased accomplishment in terms of literature and drama. All the while the stew is thickening. The time has come to shake off our fascination with celebrity for its own sake and to grasp the opportunity to claim cultural distinction. The arts have become our chief activity and we do them best because of distinctive predispositions and energies. In his time, Richard Burton had to leave Wales in order to rise in his profession. Today we have almost created the circumstances in which theatrical and cinematic excellence can be achieved in Wales. In an earlier industrial era the Welsh made the mistake of exporting products of value whilst failing to develop an infrastructure at home. There is no doubt that our contemporary actors must find their own place in the world whether that be London or Los Angeles, but if we are content merely to export our talent then a golden opportunity will have been lost. Now, as never before, a cohort of great Welsh actors is prompting Wales to say something significant about itself. The time has come for Wales to take its place alongside England and the United States as a society with a culture whose writers and actors provide daily reminders of everything that is vital and everything that is possible. Only to the degree that we complicate our own lives can we expect others to show any interest in us. Norman Mailer argued that 'we all contain the culture of our country in our un-used acting skills'. Necessarily, then, our actors hold out the promise that there is more to us than others suspect. Their accomplishments suggest that we should test them further. We may yet act Wales into history.

# Select Bibliography

David Adams, *Stage Welsh* (Llandysul: Gomer, 1996).

Philip Barnes, *A Companion to Post-War British Theatre* (New York: Barnes and Noble, 1986).

Brian Bates, *The Way of the Actor* (London: Century, 1886).

Keith Baxter, *My Sentiments Exactly* (London: Oberon, 1998).

Steven Berkoff, *I Am Hamlet* (London: Faber and Faber, 1989).

David Berry, *Wales and Cinema* (Cardiff: University of Wales Press, 1994).

Melvyn Bragg, *Rich* (London: Hodder and Stoughton, 1988).

Philip Burton, *Early Doors* (New York: Dial Press, 1969).

Michael Feeney Callan, *Anthony Hopkins: In Darkness and Light* (London: Sidgwick and Jackson, 1993).

Simon Callow, *Being an Actor* (London: Methuen, 1984).

Morris Carnovsky, *The Actor's Eye* (New York: PAJ, 1984).

Brian Cox, *Salem to Moscow* (London: Methuen, 1991).

Samuel Crow, *Shakespeare Observed* (Athens, Ohio: Ohio University Press, 1992).

W. A. Darlington, *The Actor and His Audience* (London: Phoenix, 1949).

Joanna Davies, *Taff Pac* (Talybont: Y Lolfa, 2000).

Quentin Falk, *Anthony Hopkins: Too Good To Waste* (London: Columbus, 1989).

James Fenton, *You Were Marvellous* (London: Jonathan Cape, 1973).

Richard Findlater, *Emlyn Williams* (London: Rockliff, 1956).

Richard Findlater (ed.), *At the Royal Court* (Ambergate: Amber Lane, 1981).

George McDonald Fraser, *The Hollywood History of the World* (London: Michael Joseph, 1988).

Kenneth Griffith, *Fool's Pardon* (London: Little, Brown, 1994).

Alec Guinness, *Blessings in Disguise* (London: Hamish Hamilton, 1985).

Tyrone Guthrie, *A Life in the Theatre* (London: Hamish Hamilton, 1959).

James Harding, *Emlyn Williams* (London: Weidenfeld and Nicolson, 1993).

James Harding, *Ivor Novello* (London: W. H. Allen, 1987).

Harold Hobson (ed.), *International Theatre Annual, No. 1* and *No. 3* (London: John Calder, 1956 and 1958).

Harold Hobson, *Theatre in Britain* (Oxford: Phaidon, 1984).

Richard Huggett, *Binkie Beaumont* (London: Hodder and Stoughton, 1989).

Clive James, *On Television* (London: Picador, 1991).

Graham Jenkins, *Richard Burton, My Brother* (London: Michael Joseph, 1988).

Sheila Johnston, 'Charioteers and Ploughmen', in Martyn Auty and Nick Roddick (eds), *British Cinema Now* (London: BFI, 1985).

Dedwydd Jones, *Black Book on the Welsh Theatre* (Lausanne: Iolo, 1985).

Pauline Kael, *5001 Nights at the Movies* (London: Hamish Hamilton, 1982).

Roger Lewis, *Stage People* (London: Weidenfeld and Nicolson, 1989).

Roger Lewis, *The Life and Death of Peter Sellers* (London: Century, 1994).

Tirzah Lowen, *Peter Hall Directs Antony and Cleopatra* (London: Methuen, 1990).

Brian McFarlane (ed.), *An Autobiography of British Cinema* (London: Methuen, 1997).

Micheál Mac Liammóir, 'The Light of Many Lamps', in Anthony Curtis (ed.), *The Rise and Fall of the Matinée Idol* (London: Weidenfeld and Nicolson, 1974).

Ian McIntyre, *Garrick* (London: Allen Lane, 1999).

Geoffrey Macnab, *Searching for Stars* (London: Cassell, 2000).

Norman Mailer, 'A Transit to Narcissus', in Bernardo Bertolucci, *Last Tango in Paris* (London: Plexus, 1976).

Brian Masters, *Thunder in the Air: Great Actors in Great Roles* (London: Oberon, 2000).

Robin May, *History of the Theatre* (London: Hamlyn, 1986).

John Miller, *Judi Dench: With a Crack in her Voice* (London: Weidenfeld and Nicolson, 1998).

Ethan Mordden, *Fireside Companion to Theatre* (New York: Simon and Schuster, 1988).

Sheridan Morley, *The Great Stage Stars* (London: Angus and Robertson, 1986).

Benedict Nightingale, *Fifth Row Center* (New York: Times, 1986).

Peter Noble, *Ivor Novello* (London: Falcon, 1951).

John Osborne, *Damn You, England* (London: Faber and Faber, 1994).

Terrence Pettigrew, *British Film Character Actors* (Newton Abbott: David and Charles, 1982).

Siân Phillips, *Private Faces* (London: Hodder and Stoughton, 1999).

Siân Phillips, *Public Places* (London; Hodder and Stoughton, 2000).

Cecil Price, *The English Theatre in Wales in the Eighteenth and Early Nineteenth Centuries* (Cardiff: University of Wales Press, 1948).

Rachel Roberts (ed. Alexander Walker), *No Bells on Sunday* (London: Pavilion, 1984).

Randy Roberts and James S. Olson, *John Wayne: American* (New York: The Free Press, 1995).

Ken Russell, *The Lion Roars* (London: Hutchinson, 1993).

Gamini Salgado, *King Lear, Text and Performance* (London: Macmillan, 1984).

Dominic Shellard, *British Theatre since the War* (London: Yale, 1999).

Anthony Sher, *Year of the King* (London: Chatto and Windus, 1985).

Peter Stead, *Film and the Working Class* (London: Routledge, 1989).

Peter Stead, *Richard Burton: So Much, So Little* (Bridgend: Seren, 1991).

Robert Stephens, *Knight Errant* (London: Hodder and Stoughton, 1995).

Anthony Storey, *Stanley Baker: Portrait of an Actor* (London: W. H. Allen, 1977).

Anna-Marie Taylor (ed.), *Staging Wales* (Cardiff: University of Wales Press, 1997).

David Thomson, *A Biographical Dictionary of the Cinema* (London: Secker and Warburg, 1975).

J. C. Trewin, *The English Theatre* (London: Paul Elek, 1948).

J. C. Trewin, *Five and Eighty Hamlets* (London: Hutchinson, 1982).

Harriet Walter, *Other People's Shoes* (London: Viking, 1999).

Irving Wardle, *Theatre Criticism* (London: Routledge, 1992).

Paul Webb, *Ivor Novello* (London: Stage Directions, 1999).

T. F. Wharton, *Henry the Fourth, Text and Performance* (London: Macmillan, 1983).

Emlyn Williams, *George* (London: Hamish Hamilton, 1961).

Emlyn Williams, *Emlyn* (London: The Bodley Head, 1973).

Garry Wills, *John Wayne: The Politics of Celebrity* (New York: Simon and Schuster, 1997).

Sandy Wilson, *Ivor* (London: Michael Joseph, 1975).

T. C. Worsley, *The Fugitive Art* (London: John Lehmann, 1952).

# Index